HOW WINNING LEADERS CLOSE
PERFORMANCE GAPS

MARKTHIENES
BRIANBROCKHOFF

5TH ANNIVERSARY EDITION

UNIVERSAL-PUBLISHERS
BOCA RATON FLORIDA

Gapology: How Winning Leaders Close Performance Gaps,
5th Anniversary Edition

Universal-Publishers
Boca Raton, Florida | USA

ISBN-10: 1-62734-030-0
ISBN-13: 978-1-62734-030-4

www.universal-publishers.com

The Library of Congress has cataloged the 1st edition as follows:

Thienes, Mark, 1957-
Gapology : how winning leaders close performance gaps / Mark Thienes, with Brian Brockhoff.
p. cm.
Includes bibliographical references and index.
ISBN-13: 978-1-59942-855-0 (pbk. : alk. paper)
ISBN-10: 1-59942-855-5 (pbk. : alk. paper)
1. Performance--Management. 2. Performance standards. 3. Senior leadership teams--Management. 4. Leadership. I. Brockhoff, Brian, 1966- II. Title.
HF5549.5.P37T55 2010
658.3'128--dc22

2010007908

Website: www.gapologyinstitute.com

CONTENTS

FOREWORD

MIND THE GAP

A few years ago, when my husband studied for a semester in England, my son, Joe, and I went to visit him for a week.

We traveled throughout London using the city's subway system, the Underground or "Tube." There was a significant space between the station platform and the trains. As a safety precaution, a recorded announcement repeatedly told travelers to "Mind the Gap!" Since this was our primary mode of transportation, we heard this message over and over! Before long, we found ourselves telling each other to "Mind the Gap!" When I got back to work after my trip, I had to smile when I noticed one of my colleagues had a "Mind the Gap!" bumper sticker in her office. She, too, had been struck by this message while visiting London.

"I highly recommend this book to all business professionals who expect exceptional performance."

Now, after reading *Gapology*, "Mind the Gap!" has taken on a new—and much more relevant—meaning.

My career has spanned more than thirty years and encompassed leadership positions in operations, human resources, and learning and development with sever-

1

al national retail concepts. I have had responsibility for all three of these areas at Buffalo Wild Wings, Inc., where, since 2001, I've had the privilege of helping the company evolve into a high-performing, goal-oriented company with a history of achieving year-over-year growth.

Gapology captures the essence of many of the business challenges I have encountered during my career. More importantly, it provides strategies for developing solutions to close (and seal up) these Performance Gaps.

Sometimes in the heat of the battle, we lose sight of the methodical and logical processes that assure high performance. *Gapology* solves that!

Mark Thienes and Brian Brockhoff have done an exceptional job of simply and practically explaining how winning leaders perform—and help others perform—by identifying and closing gaps.

Trust me, Mark knows gaps. When I first met him, he was already a rock star. The company we worked for was going through major changes, shifting away from a culture where many things were mandated, with little need for managers to make decisions, and evolving into a culture that required leaders to take responsibility and make decisions on their own. Many resisted the change. In this stressed environment, Mark was a breath of fresh air. He made things happen. If he needed something that did not exist, he didn't complain; instead, he created it. Mark was clearly a top performer—a winning leader! Even back then, he was a cross between a surgeon and an artist when it came to identifying and closing Performance Gaps.

Mark was our "Maddy."

I have always been compelled to assess where and why there are gaps in performance. Who is doing well? Who is not? How can we get the low performers to replicate what the superstars are doing? How do we perform compared to our goals? Why or why aren't we achieving expectations? Most importantly, how do we help people accomplish their goals—and the company's?

Sometimes gaps are obvious. A staff person once came into my office to inform me that field managers were not following a certain reporting procedure.

I asked how the field managers would know what they should be doing. The reply: a memo outlining the process was sent out several months earlier. However, there had been no follow-up communication. Obviously, we had a Knowledge Gap.

It is understandable that gaps happen, as long as you can identify them and implement a plan to fix them. In this particular case, once we identified the gap about communicating the reporting procedure, we were able to take action to fix it.

Since reviewing the draft copy of this book, I have started applying *Gapology* to the personal, as well as the business, aspects of my life. If I am not meeting an expectation I set for myself—getting to the next belt level in karate or reorganizing that spare room in my house—I find myself asking, "What is the gap and how do I close it?"

Gapology does not just explain how to identify gaps; it explains how to implement solutions to close the gaps to achieve results. Mark and Brian have captured a simple but profound concept: winning leaders close gaps, and that is why they are winning leaders.

I highly recommend this book to all business professionals who expect exceptional performance from themselves and their teams. This book should be read cover to cover. It will likely become a much-used reference tool as new gaps arise and new solutions are needed. The "Maddy Stories" will make great individual training or teaching modules.

And you'll save both time and money by not having to travel to London to learn how to "Mind the Gap!"

JUDY SHOULAK

EVP, PRESIDENT NORTH AMERICA
BUFFALO WILD WINGS

PROLOGUE
MADDY'S STORY

As was the custom at the annual awards banquet of the XYZ Solutions Company, the final and most prestigious award was saved until after dinner. The wait staff scurried to gather the last of the dessert plates, wine glasses, and coffee cups from the estimated four hundred black-tie-and-evening-gown-clad district managers, sales managers, sales reps, and company executives, as an announcement came over the sound system: "The award for XYZ's District Manager of the Year will be announced in five minutes. Please return to your seats."

"Maddy and her team have put together a three-year run unlike any I have ever seen."

-Tom Case CEO XYZ

Each of the three regions that make up the sales force of XYZ has good reason to be proud of its top performing district manager, but of the thirty district managers, only one stood out as the obvious front-runner.

Excitement was thick in the air, but not in anticipation as to which district manager would be crowned that night. No, they already knew that. The anticipation was about what she might share with the team as to her unbelievable run of performance. How had she done it? And will her mere words have the power to further propel the company forward? History was being made that night at XYZ. District performance of this magnitude was clearly the best in the industry, and that meant XYZ was also moving to the top of the industry in market share. Everybody loves to work for a winner, and XYZ was now poised to benefit even more from the wisdom of Madeline Ferguson.

XYZ kept the final year-end results sealed until the awards banquet was held. In a closed-door meeting, the company's top executives conducted a comprehensive review of the results, and each cast his or her vote for District Manager of the Year. Thomas Case, president and CEO of XYZ, received the votes and made the final decision. It is not known how many votes Case granted himself, but he was known as a fair man, so his final decision would never be questioned. But, this year there was very little that could be questioned.

Soon the lights of the Marriott ballroom dimmed, and the spotlights lit up the stage and podium while the disc jockey blasted Tina Turner's song, *The Best*. The crowd cheered and clapped to the beat. Carefully placed on the table behind the podium on the stage sat a single glass trophy cloaked in a linen cloth. The most prized honor at XYZ was receiving that piece of glass. It was quite impressive in size and had become the source of career growth and the subject of legend.

Case waited for his cue, and as the song ended he stood from his position at the front table and walked to the side of the stage, then up three steps and across the stage to the podium. The spotlight followed him, and anyone who was not already standing and rocking to the music was now on his or her feet giving Case a standing ovation. He is wildly popular, and XYZ is known as a great place to work. He tapped the microphone and asked the three region managers to join him on the stage. Amid the applause and shouting, all made their way through the crowd, assembling in a row behind Case. He raised his hands to quell the cheering and applause

"I always wanted to be a rock star," he said as the crowd laughed and began to simmer somewhere above a boil. Case began, "I want to congratulate all of tonight's winners. In what was a challenging year for our company and the industry, you made us proud! I want to give special thanks to the three district managers who took the top regional awards earlier tonight. You have separated yourselves from your peers and made significant contributions to our company's performance this year. It is now time for one of you to be named District Manager of the Year!" The crowd erupted into a thunderous roar.

Case continued, "I would ask that you hold your applause until the end of my announcement. Although this is a time to celebrate, I consider my remarks this evening to be especially important." He paused, then continued, "Greatness in results is something we all must understand and strive for, but in today's challenging economy, greatness in results carries a special meaning. I request that our 'District Manager of the Year' remain seated until the conclusion of my remarks, while, of course, basking in the spotlight of our unwavering admiration." Everyone laughed and cheered.

"Without further rambling, let's get to it," Case added, followed by another round of screaming applause. "Our District Manager of the Year, for the third straight year, is Madeline Ferguson!" Although asked to hold their applause, the central region bursts out loud for their hero, but they quickly gained their composure.

"Maddy, as we all know her, joined XYZ just a little over three years ago, taking over one of the toughest markets in the company. After getting her feet on the ground, she had a company-leading first year, even though the first few months were tough. That was followed by a totally dominant second year. Since then, there has been no looking back for Maddy and her team. She has put together a three-year run unlike any I have ever seen. Maddy, we are humbled and honored by your performance," Case added, making a partial bow in Maddy's direction. Maddy beamed with a glow that resembled the planet Mars.

Case paused to take a drink of water, obviously choked up, while applause and catcalls rang out. Guests sitting at the front tables could see a tear well up in his eyes. "Maddy's result improvements this past year have spanned all measurable categories and are truly remarkable. Her district achieved the following:

#1 in sales to plan!
#1 in profit to plan!
#1 in customer satisfaction!
#1 in lowest team turnover with two of her ten sales managers promoted to district manager! Outstanding!
#1 in community fund-raising and top volunteerism!"

Following a pregnant pause, Case added, "All of these achievements have come from a district manager who openly shares her winning tactics with anyone who will listen. Maddy joined XYZ after a very successful career as both a district and region manager for another sales organization. Anyone who has visited her office and has seen her trophy case of awards garnered from years of successful leadership knows that we are blessed by her presence."

Case paused and wiped his eyes, clearly feeling an emotional connection to Maddy's performance. He continued, "Maddy knows how to win. You've heard her say it time after time. She simply identifies and closes Performance Gaps in herself and her team. This is not a one-time process, but it is her daily behavior. It is a skill that she has honed to perfection and spread to her team. She practices closing Performance Gaps daily and applies these very fundamental tactics to everything that requires great execution.

"You may have heard Maddy comment when asked why she was so successful in a specific promotion or event, 'Oh, that was just a Knowledge Gap that we identified and closed, or we found an Importance Gap in our team. We were able to close that one quickly.' Or, 'It was an Action Gap in a few of the sales managers, and once we closed it, the ball was in their court.' The bottom line is that Maddy gets out of bed every morning and proceeds to identify and close Performance Gaps in herself and her team. She is truly the original Gapologist!" Case concluded.

"So tonight we have a special surprise for each of you." The crowd gasped, and with those words, a white-jacket-clad waiter stepped up to each of the sixty round tables and handed each guest a copy of a white-and-black-covered book entitled *Gapology*.

"As has been our custom, the District Manager of the Year is asked to share his or her keys to success upon receiving the award on stage. For the past two years, Maddy has stepped up to this mike and talked about closing Performance Gaps. So about six months ago, I invited Maddy to the home office for a couple of weeks. Working with my close friends and winning leader experts, Mark Thienes and Brian Brockhoff, we picked Maddy's brain, gathering and documenting all of her Performance Gap identification and closure examples."

"We blended Maddy's life experiences with examples from her sales team at XYZ and have included them in Mark and Brian's new book, *Gapology—How Winning Leaders Close Performance Gaps*. Mark and Brian have done extensive studies of winning leaders and found their common thread is in identifying and closing Performance Gaps in their teams.

"Each of you is fortunate because you have just received the first printing of *Gapology,* which includes everything you will need to identify and close Performance Gaps. My expectation is that each of you will use *Gapology* to achieve excellence in execution and unparalleled results, regardless of your role. We want a big gap between XYZ and the competition!" The XYZ team went into a frenzy with a mixture of screams, shouts, and applause.

Case continued, "I did a little math, which may not surprise any of you who know me well. If each of our thirty district managers had performed at the same level as Maddy for the past year, we would have added twenty million dollars to our bottom line profit!

"So we need everyone at XYZ to become a Gapologist, identifying and closing Performance Gaps in your teams, your processes, and yourself! Let's make this the greatest year in XYZ's history!"

Everyone jumped to his or her feet, applauding and cheering. "Maddy, come on down!" Case shouted as the disc jockey cranks up *Celebration* by Kool and the Gang. Maddy, impeded with high-fives, fist bumps, a few hugs, and a dozen handshakes or so, slowly made her victory walk to the stage to garner her third glass trophy.

The standing ovation and cheering seemed like it would never end. This night became legendary in the history of XYZ, and most say it was the turning point that propelled the company into the industry-leading position it currently holds.

After accepting the trophy and shaking hands with Tom and the region managers, Maddy remained on stage as Case stepped back to the mike and said, "One thing before you go and celebrate the night away. Take it easy on Maddy tonight! Remember, we start the leadership workshops promptly at eight o'clock in the morning."

Everyone laughed and some moaned. "By the way," Case added. "I have good news for all of the district managers out there. Maddy has won her last District Manager of the Year Award!"

The crowd gasped. "That's right... effective next week, Maddy is our newest region manager!" The crowd erupted once again for what felt like an eternity.

"Our expansion plans are on track, and we look forward to our star Gapologist contributing at a higher level, and giving these three" pointing to the region managers, "a real run for their money!"

Case concluded, "Good luck to all of my new Gapologists! Go forth and, identify and close those Performance Gaps!"

INTRODUCTION
PERFORMANCE GAPS

Gaps happen.

They happen in every company, department, work team, and individual performer every day.

We experience gaps when we call for cable service, try to renew our driver's license, shop for groceries, or sign up for health insurance. As customers, we are so often the victims of gaps in our everyday lives that we have learned to just accept them. We rarely even complain. We just suck it up and settle.

"Gapology will certainly change your results and it has the power to change your life!"

Gaps are everywhere.

They always have been and will always be a part of our lives, but as the world has become more complex, the number and frequency of gaps has grown exponentially. They happen in the private sector, the public sector, and nonprofit organizations.

Gaps account for trillions of dollars of lost revenue and profit each year.

Most gaps are simply the result of someone not taking an action that should have been taken. These are what we call Performance Gaps.

Performance Gaps are the number-one risk to all companies and organizations today. By contrast, leaders and teams that have the fewest gaps and close those gaps quickest win. They win by big margins.

Our research shows that winning leaders anticipate Performance Gaps and prevent them, but when gaps do occur, they close them quickly. Winning leaders close Performance Gaps by taking action and moving their teams to take action. Taking the right action is key to closing Performance Gaps.

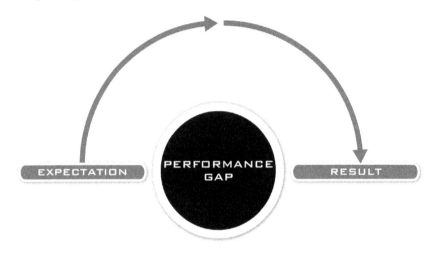

FIGURE 1 - PERFORMANCE GAP MODEL

In Figure 1, the Performance Gap Model, you will see that Performance Gaps are the gaps between what you expect and the actual outcome. Performance Gaps are gaps in behavior that create gaps in results.

Winning leaders spend a significant amount of time observing their team's behavior, comparing that behavior to the expectation. They then compare the actual results produced to the result expectations. This directly connects the behaviors to the results and highlights any Performance Gaps. The better the behavior, the better the results. Gaps in behavior create gaps in results. As you compare behavioral expectations with actual behavior, you will not only see the Performance Gaps, but you will also have the opportunity to see excellence and thus have the opportunity for reinforcement and recognition. Winning leaders consistently connect behavior and results.

Gapology is the term we developed to describe what winning leaders do to identify and close Performance Gaps in their teams. Gapology is their process. For a
decade, we analyzed the results, leadership behaviors, and tactics of winning
leaders as compared to those of leaders who were not winning. We wanted to
understand how winning leaders win and if winning could be replicated, and we
were curious about whether winning can be taught to those not winning or if it is
something that winning leaders are born with.

We had a laboratory of about 1,000 leaders, and over the course of a decade we
interacted with these leaders, analyzed their result trends, contrasted their results with each other, and documented trends, all in hopes of eventually understanding what winning is really made of. You might say we dissected winning to
find out what was inside.

To accomplish this, we interviewed both winning leaders and those not winning,
trying to understand their leadership traits and behaviors, as well as what tactics
the winning leaders employ in order to win, what accountability measures they
apply to create a winning team, and what prioritization mechanisms are in place.
Also, how do these leaders define winning and communicate winning expectations to their teams? What are the gaps between winning and not winning?

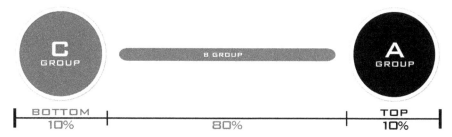

FIGURE 2 - ABC GROUPS

We limited the sample group to the top 10 percent in performance, the A-
Group, and the bottom 10 percent in performance, the C-Group. See Figure 2.
The A-Group, we also refer to as the "winning leaders," and the C-Group as the
"not winning leaders." We wanted to understand the difference between these
true outlying performance groups. The middle 80 percent, the B-Group, was not
the focus of our study. The A-Group allows us to see the potential of all groups,
and the C-Group allows us to measure lost performance. As we juxtapose the
two, we gain insight into the possibilities of overall performance.

To determine their performance, we looked only at the leader's five most directly controllable and comparable metrics:

- Sales to budget (P&L)

- Profit to budget (P&L)

- Customer satisfaction (on-going survey scores)

- Team satisfaction (annual survey)

- Team turnover (annual rate)

These metrics also aligned with their annual performance measures, thus providing a level playing field and best way to define "winning" for the leaders measured.

As you might expect, the gap in results between the A-Group and the C-Group in our study was very large! Unfortunately, the performance of the winning leaders was literally being canceled out by the poor performance of those not winning; The C-Group canceled out the positive performance of the A-Group. Because of this, the performance of the total team was limited to the performance of the middle, the B-Group. The entire team therefore, becomes essentially a B-Group in performance, you might say mediocre. While we view this as unacceptable, we did not see it as insurmountable. The C-Group just needed to learn what the A-Group was doing differently, and they needed to do it fast!

The C-Group needed to understand and execute Gapology.

At first it wasn't totally clear why the gap was so great between the A-Group and C-Group. After all, both groups were given the same instruction, had access to the same tools and resources, and therefore had the same opportunity for success. Why were their results so dramatically different?

The reason for the gap became more clearly defined when the leadership behaviors and tactics of the A- and C-Groups were observed. The A-Group shared a common thread. They moved to action by identifying and closing Performance Gaps in themselves and in their teams. Without knowing it and without a common playbook, the A-Group followed a similar sequential path to winning that is not present in the C-Group. The sequential path the winning leaders followed is what we came to call Gapology. Now we knew, in part, why their performance was so different. It was all about taking action, the right action, and teaching their teams to do the same. Think about the magnitude of this for a moment. Regardless of their background, level of education, geographic location, gender, or race, winning leaders consistently identified and then closed Performance Gaps in themselves and their teams! Wow, this was their secret!

When we first saw this amazing thread emerge it was like we had stumbled upon King Tut's tomb. The ultimate key to winning was staring us in the face. Winning leaders identify and close Performance Gaps! They do so by moving their teams to take the right actions consistently. The right actions then drive performance and results. We saw that winning performance can be taught to all leaders and therefore winning can be replicated! This is where we discovered and named the winning leader process Gapology!

Our excitement waned for a moment as we realized that we needed to tackle an even bigger question: What tactics do winning leaders use to close and prevent Performance Gaps? We needed to identify the Root Solutions that winning leaders apply in order to teach all leaders to win. And that became the simple mission of the book; to present to the world how winning leaders win! We figured it out, and all of the winning leader methods can now be yours!

As we interviewed and documented our conversations with winning leaders, we found commonalities. The most amazing was that all Performance Gaps are Knowledge, Importance, Action, or some combination of the three. This makes identifying and then closing Performance Gaps easier. Once you have identified a gap, you can close it.

See Figure 3, Performance Gap Types.

We knew we were onto something big and potentially life changing because we could teach Gapology. The secret to winning on a consistent basis was coming clearly into view!

FIGURE 3 - PERFORMANCE GAP TYPES

KNOWLEDGE GAPS
THE "WHAT" AND THE "HOW"

Winning leaders ensure that their teams know "what" actions to take and then "how" to do them. They spend exhaustive time ensuring that there aren't any Knowledge Gaps in their teams. This may sound pretty basic, and it is, but most Performance Gaps start as Knowledge Gaps. In contrast, it is very clear that the C-Group routinely overlooks Knowledge Gaps, assuming their teams are clear on the "what" and the "how."

Knowledge Gaps are the most common and the most costly Performance Gaps!

IMPORTANCE GAPS
THE "WHY" AND THE "WHEN"

Winning leaders ensure that their teams know "why" an action is important and "when" it must be done. They find that explaining the "why" to their teams is a game-changer, an engagement driver, and that their teams are more likely to take an action when they know why it matters. This makes their actions more important, improves performance, and increases job satisfaction.

Winning leaders also find that they can't overlook "when" an action must be taken. "When" something must be done matters. Timing and prioritization of actions matter and are critical.

Once again, we found that the contrast between the A-Group and the C-Group is huge. The C-Group leaders miss expectations routinely because they leave out the "why" and have a "just do it" mentality. They underestimate the impact that "why" has on their team's behavior. For these leaders, the explanation of "why" is the exception and certainly not the rule. The C-Group is also loose on the clarity of "when" an action must be taken, assuming it is known. This creates recurring Performance Gaps!

ACTION GAPS
THE "CHOICE"

Action Gaps mean that despite knowing "what" to do and "how" to do it, despite knowing "why" it is critical and "when" it must be done, the right actions are not taken. Ouch! Winning leaders do not accept Action Gaps. They go after them aggressively and close these gaps. They apply strong Root Solutions to prevent these gaps and close them when they do occur. In contrast, leaders who are not winning come up short here, often expressing frustration with their team's inaction or incorrect action. The C-Group leaders suffer from excessive Action Gaps, often blaming their team, when it is their own lack of leadership that is the biggest issue.

Winning leaders know that Action Gaps are the most difficult to close and devote the time and attention necessary to ensure that they are closed air tight.

We devoted a significant portion of our study to understanding the methods winning leaders use to close and prevent Performance Gaps. We call these methods Root Solutions. We divide them into Knowledge Gap Root Solutions, Importance Gap Root Solutions, and Action Gap Root Solutions. We have identified the top three Root Solutions for each type of gap. These Root Solutions can be immediately added to your toolbox to improve your effectiveness as a leader.

We found that Gapology is both the mindset and the leadership rhythm of winning leaders. It is their instinctive problem-solving methodology and problem-prevention tool. Gapology can be applied proactively before an event or project to ensure gaps do not occur. It can also be used after the fact to autopsy outcomes that have already occurred, gaining an understanding of the wins and the breakdowns (Performance Gaps).

Gapology is a powerful tool that will transform team culture, creating a bias for action. It changes how individuals, teams, and organizations think, speak, and behave. Once you, as the leader of a team, become a true "Gapologist," you can accomplish results far beyond your peers or competitors, joining that elite group of what we call winning leaders or the A-Group. We have seen many examples of this and have even seen examples of the C-Group performers moving to the top 10 percent!

Gapology can be taught and will spread throughout your organization, as well as become a source of great personal development for those who learn to apply it.

Once your eyes and your mind are open to Gapology, your life as a leader will be changed forever. You will see things you didn't see before. It will influence what you hear when having conversations with your team. It will shape your actions following the analysis of results. You will begin seeing gaps everywhere, even outside of your professional life. Be careful or you might find yourself walking around in a trance mumbling, "I see gaps..." This happened to us as we went through the journey of gathering the data for our case study. We began to see gaps everywhere.

So, proceed with caution. You can get overwhelmed with the sheer number of gaps. Pick your battles by prioritizing the Performance Gaps. Go after those with the biggest payback.

As a leader, you will often find that you are the gap or, at least, the source of the gap. Your behavior may actually be hindering the performance of your team. Be prepared and open to looking in the mirror. Gapology, identifying and closing Performance Gaps, can appear deceptively simple so don't be fooled. Winning leaders make winning look easy, but that is often the outcome of significant learning through trial and error. Winning leaders learn from their failures. They don't fear failure, and they don't get frustrated and give up. They simply identify and close Performance Gaps, and each time they learn and grow from the process.

FIGURE 4 - GAP CLOSURE SEQUENCE

This is easy to remember. Think K-I-A, like KIA, the car company.

Winning leaders showed us that the sequence matters. See Figure 4, the Gap Closure Sequence. You can't close Action Gaps without Knowledge and Importance Gaps being closed. It won't work. Closing Action Gaps requires knowledge and realizing the importance of the action to be in place. So keep it simple: close Knowledge Gaps, then Importance Gaps, and then Action Gaps. Often, by simply closing the Knowledge Gaps, action takes place, but it is not sustained without the importance of the action being understood.

Consider the following a sequential example of closing Performance Gaps in your team:

- "My team knows what to do and how to do it." Knowledge Gaps closed.

- "My team knows why it must be done and when it must be done." Importance Gaps closed.

- "My team makes the choice to take action and achieves the expected outcome." Actions Gaps closed.

This sequential flow ensures gaps are closed. It can be used either proactively to prevent gaps or after the gaps have been created to close them. As you enter a project, event, or change initiative, use this flow to measure gap closure in advance of launch date.

HOW TO USE THIS BOOK

Gapology, the book, also flows from left to right in gap order as detailed in Figure 4. The book is divided into four parts: **Knowledge Gaps**, **Importance Gaps**, **Action Gaps**, and **Next Steps**. The first three parts include: Performance Gap diagrams, explanations of the gaps, Root Solutions to each gap, examples of what the gaps look like in Maddy's team, "stories and learnings" from Maddy's sales career that apply directly to the gaps, and the leader behaviors to identify and close gaps. There are also numerous exercises specific to identifying and closing gaps in your own team.

Gapology is for all leaders and professionals regardless of the size of the team you lead or the industry in which you work. Much of the learning will likely be your own self-discovery. We wrote *Gapology* to share the tremendous impact that closing gaps has on the performance of winning leaders. As we have shared, the Performance Gap between winning leaders and those not winning is huge. We refer to it privately as the Grand Canyon. Winning leaders, the A-Group, stand on one side of the canyon, and the C-Group stands hopelessly on the other side unable to see the bridge (Gapology) to get across.

Gapology is the bridge that leads from failure to success, and winning leaders cross that bridge many times each day. When learned and applied, Gapology causes a mindset shift in leaders and is, by far, the most significant performance game-changer we have ever experienced. It gives you the ability to look back at specific outcomes and accurately determine what went right and wrong, while also giving you the ability to look forward and anticipate gaps, thus allowing you to perform at much higher levels.

For simplicity in this book, we use the terms "leader," "team member," and "customer" to describe the roles where Performance Gaps occur. You can modify these terms to fit the roles applicable to your organization.

"Leader" refers to anyone in a leadership role within a team or organization. This includes professionals in individual contributor roles.

As we have stated, "winning leaders" are defined as the top 10 percent of performers in our study. We also call them the A-Group. Leaders that are in the bottom 10 percent of performers are also called the C-Group.

"Team member" is anyone in a subordinate role to the leader. These are the players on a team.

"Customer" refers to anyone the leader or team member is working to influence, so they may be an actual customer in the traditional service model or a charitable donor to a nonprofit organization. This term includes the clients and patients and anyone on the receiving end of a service provided.

We use the term "Root Solution" to describe the methodology winning leaders use to close Performance Gaps. This term is similar to a "root cause" of a Performance Gap, but we approach it from the standpoint of closing gaps and solving problems, thus "Root Solution."

As you read *Gapology* you will find that Maddy is our example of a winning leader. What we don't emphasize is that she was not always a winning leader. As she learned to apply Gapology and began to identify and close Performance Gaps in herself and her team, she became a winning leader. For the purpose of example and explanation of gaps, we use Maddy's process of discovering and leveraging Gapology as district manager in the sales industry.

You will learn from Maddy's gap identification and closure methods and be able to apply them to your team. Her stories are real. They are representative of the real discoveries from the winning leaders in our research.

Please refer to the XYZ Organizational Structure, Figure 5. This lays out the simple structure of the XYZ sales division. It will help you understand many of the examples we use. Organizational structure can be the source of many gaps, so it is critical to keep in mind as you consider the Root Solutions to gaps.

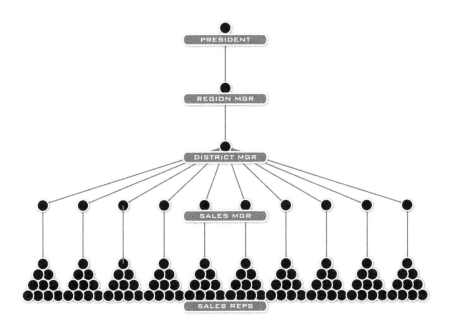

FIGURE 5 - XYZ ORGANIZATIONAL STRUCTURE

Here is an example of Performance Gaps in Maddy's team:

Maddy's team of ten sales managers was expected to produce $5 million in sales revenue in period one of the year, but produced only $4.5 million. The team, therefore, has a gap in results of $500,000. This is a Performance Gap in results. Maddy is likely to have additional Performance Gaps in her behavior and the behavior of her team that led to the Performance Gap in results.

The identification of the Performance Gaps in Maddy's team starts when she asks these four key questions:

- Why did we miss our sales plan by $500,000?

- Which sales managers made their sales plan, and what did they do differently than those who missed?

- Which sales reps made their sales plan, and what did they do differently than those who missed?

- What actions must we take to make our sales plan in period two, plus make up the $500,000 gap from period one?

The answers to these and the key follow-up questions will uncover the gaps Maddy's team is facing. Gaps must be identified and closed at the behavioral level. Once the behaviors are identified, Maddy and her team can apply the correct Root Solutions to close each gap. She must work with a high sense of urgency, because the team already missed its sales plan in period one. The sales miss in period one predicts a sales budget miss in period two, unless the behaviors that created the original miss have changed. Her team must look back to period one and identify the Performance Gaps, while looking forward to periods two, three, and beyond to close the gaps. Her success in the role of district manager depends on her speed and efficiency in executing this process.

Gapology is the most critical tool in a leader's toolbox. Practice this process over and over again, plus teach it to your team, so they are closing gaps before you even see them.

Review the Gapology Model, Figure 6. This represents the full Gapology process, including the Root Solutions that winning leaders use to identify and close Performance Gaps. Memorize this model.

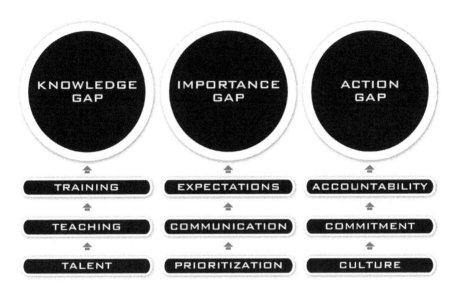

FIGURE 6 - GAPOLOGY MODEL

Gapology, the book, is devoted to teaching you how to use the Gapology Model, so you can become a true Gapologist just like Maddy. Each of the Root Solutions pictured in Figure 6 has been tested and proven successful by winning leaders. Gapology is a powerful tool, and now it is yours. So, strap on your helmet, buckle your seat belt, and let's go!

Gapology will certainly change your results, and it has the power to change your life!

25

PART **1**

KNOWLEDGE GAPS

1

IDENTIFYING
KNOWLEDGE GAPS

Knowledge Gaps are the gaps between what we don't know and what we do know.

This sounds simple, doesn't it? Knowledge Gaps are the simplest gaps to overcome, but in today's complex world Knowledge Gaps are often overlooked and certainly underestimated.

Knowledge Gaps are the result of either a lack of knowledge or a lack of skill. Many leaders focus only on providing knowledge and ignore developing and validating skills. Winning leaders do not make this mistake.

"Knowledge Gaps are the result of either a lack of knowledge or a lack of skill."

Here are the simple questions to identify Knowledge Gaps in a team:

- Do your team members know what to do?

- Do they know how to do it?

- Can they demonstrate and repeat the behavior?

Closing Knowledge Gaps is the first step in great performance. Most often, the lowest-level team member is directly interfacing with the customer and is therefore responsible for taking the correct action. Knowledge Gaps can be devastating to performance here. Closing a Knowledge Gap can often be as simple as having the team member demonstrate and practice the desired behavior. During this time, the leader's behavior should be to encourage, coach, and recognize the team member's actions until the desired behavior becomes habit. Combine this with setting clear expectations that the behavior is to be repeated, and you are well on your way to closing this Knowledge Gap.

Some leaders make the mistake of assuming that their team members know a behavior because they have been trained. They compound the mistake thinking a behavior will be sustained.

CAUTION: Performance Gaps ahead!

To illustrate Knowledge Gaps, let's return to the example from Maddy's team used in the Introduction. As you may recall, Maddy is the district manager overseeing ten sales managers, each with ten sales reps. Together, they are responsible for producing $5 million in revenue during period one. Her team produced only $4.5 million, thus a gap of $500,000 in sales.

See Figure 7, a chart that illustrates Maddy's team results for period one:

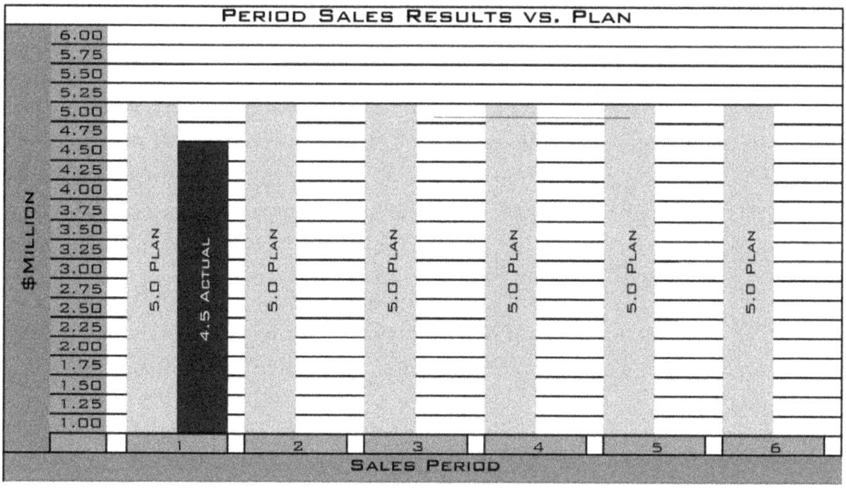

FIGURE 7 - PERIOD ONE SALES

Immediately following the end of period one, Maddy gathered the ten sales managers together in a meeting to determine the Performance Gaps that caused the sales miss.

She facilitated an autopsy of period one by asking the following questions:

- Why did we miss our sales plan by $500,000?

- Which sales managers made their sales plan, and what did they do differently than those who missed?

- Which sales reps made their sales plan, and what did they do differently than those who missed?

- What actions must we take to make our sales plan in period two, plus make up the $500,000 gap from period one?

While listening to the sales managers' answers, she confirmed that the sales manager team had developed and introduced a new three-step selling process, which was to be fully implemented and in use by all sales reps during period one. This new selling process had been thoroughly tested during the last quarter. It was designed to ensure the achievement of the $5 million sales plan in period one and to then exceed plan for the rest of the year.

However, she is reminded that four of the sales managers, 40 percent of the team, were not in attendance at the meeting when the process was developed. They were copied on the new three-step process via email, but she discovered that they had not read it thoroughly. They assumed it was optional for period one and that they could catch up later. They did not fully execute the new three-step process and had not taught it to their sales reps.

The six sales managers who executed the new three-step process exceeded sales plan by a combined $200,000, and they were the same six sales managers who developed the process. The four who were not part of the meeting missed sales plan by a combined $700,000. Had these four sales managers just made their sales plan, Maddy's team would have achieved $5.2 million in sales for period one and exceeded the plan by $200,000.

Maddy has now identified significant Knowledge Gaps that were a major factor in her team's poor performance and a primary reason for the $500,000 sales miss in period one.

But who has Knowledge Gaps?

Here are the facts and the Knowledge Gaps Maddy and team have uncovered:

- A new three-step selling process was developed by six of the sales managers with Maddy's input. The three-step process was shared with their sales rep teams, practiced with each rep until they could demonstrate the behavior, and declared to be an expectation of every rep with every client starting in period one. The three-step process and rollout proved successful and resulted in each of the six sales managers exceeding their sales plan in period one. No Knowledge Gaps here.

- The other four sales managers did not have full knowledge or buy-in of the three-step process. They had missed the meeting where the three-step process was developed. These four sales managers had heard of the three-step process and were copied on the process via email, but they had not read it thoroughly. Their reps were unaware of the three-step process and did not execute it during period one. Big Knowledge Gaps!

- Maddy did not review actual sales versus plan by sales manager for the first few weeks of period one. She did not publish sales by manager during the first few weeks of period one. If the sales had been reviewed and published, it should have been evident to all that the three-step process was in play in certain sales managers' areas and not in others. Any curious sales manager could have asked another sales manager why there was a big gap in sales between sales managers. Knowledge Gaps!

Do you see any other Knowledge Gaps?

Yes, there are many other Knowledge Gaps … and some of these are with Maddy herself.

Here are the gaps with the leader, Maddy:

- Maddy was unaware that her entire team was not fully engaged and executing the three-step process. She assumed (gap creator) and did not verify that every sales manager and sales rep understood the communication and was executing the process. Knowledge Gaps!

- Maddy did not complete effective sales analysis to catch the sales trend difference between the six sales managers who developed the process and the four who did not attend the meeting. Maddy's Knowledge Gaps contributed to the team's poor performance in period one because she contributed to the Knowledge Gaps in the team!

- Maddy's Knowledge Gaps have put period two at risk, because 40 percent of the team is not prepared to execute the three-step process at the beginning of period two.

The Knowledge Gaps of the leader cause Knowledge Gaps in the team, and they often go unidentified, undiscussed, and therefore go unclosed. Winning leaders show a high level of self-awareness of their own gaps. As you can see, Maddy's own Knowledge Gaps prevented the team from winning in period one and were a cause in the miss in achieving the expected results. These gaps were totally avoidable and even if missed before period one began, they could have been identified and closed as the period progressed. There was significant evidence that there were Performance Gaps with four of the sales managers, which should have sent up a red flag.

Performance Gaps manifest themselves in behavior, results, or both. The results show the gaps in behavior, and the gaps in behavior predict the gaps in results. The Performance Gaps in the four sales managers were predictable, given their lack of attendance at the meeting. Maddy should have discovered the gaps with the four sales managers prior to or early in period one by asking questions and remaining curious about their poor results. She could have visited with these sales managers and their reps, observing their behavior. It would have been evident that the three-step process was not being used in 40 percent of her district.

Maddy is acutely aware that much of the blame for the miss in period one falls on her shoulders. She makes that declaration to the team and vows to never make that mistake again. She then asks the team to declare the gaps in their behavior. They accurately admit the gaps and commit to close those gaps.

Hopefully, Maddy has now leveraged the miss in period one to strengthen the team's performance, resolve, and understanding of Gapology.

Curiosity is a key quality of winning leaders, and it is a key to identifying gaps. We have found that winning leaders are always asking why results are good and why results are bad. The answers to these simple questions lead them directly to gaps in performance because the questions and subsequent answers expose the gaps.

Gaps must first be identified if they are to be closed.

You can't close a gap you don't see!

If you don't ask questions, you become the gap!

Do leaders who speak more than listen uncover the gaps? Leaders who do not listen actively do not uncover gaps and are surprised when results miss expectations.

We discovered six distinct winning leader behaviors to identify Knowledge Gaps. As you review them, ask yourself which of these did Maddy not have in play during period one. With all six in play, she would have exceeded her sales plan.

Winning Leader Behaviors to Identify Knowledge Gaps

- *Review actual results versus expectations.*
- *Observe behavior versus expectations.*
- *Ask questions about results and behavior. Be curious.*
- *Listen to the answers completely before follow-up.*
- *Avoid blaming. Keep focused on identifying the gap.*
- *Ask confirming questions to determine the gap.*

Identifying Knowledge Gaps is the first step winning leaders use to drive great performance. Follow these six steps and you will identify the true Performance Gaps. Many leaders jump to conclusions and assume gaps that aren't evident, and this may cause them to work on closing gaps that are not the real issue. They may also spend more time assigning blame than moving the team to action. Unfortunately, this is a common behavior in leaders who are not winning, the C-Group.

If this is your behavior, you may have personal Knowledge Gaps to work on. You can see how Maddy's knowledge of gaps in herself and her team position her to close the gaps quickly and move the team to achieving the sales plan.

The gaps she has identified in herself are invaluable. Leaders are very often the reason for Performance Gaps in their teams. Maddy was a major part of the gaps in this case. She has learned a big lesson from the period one miss and will not let it happen again. Great leaders learn from their mistakes and do not repeat them. As you will learn, Maddy is a great leader, but she still has a lot to learn.

GAPOLOGY LESSONS
IDENTIFYING KNOWLEDGE GAPS

Knowledge Gaps are the gaps between what we don't know and what we do know.

Knowledge Gaps are the result of either a lack of knowledge or a lack of skill. Many leaders focus only on providing knowledge and ignore developing and validating skills. Winning leaders do not make this mistake.

Curiosity is a key quality of winning leaders, and it is a key to identifying gaps. We have found that winning leaders are always asking why results are good and why results are bad. The answers to these simple questions lead them directly to gaps in performance because the questions and subsequent answers expose the gaps.

You can't close a gap you don't see!

If you don't ask questions, you become the gap!

Winning Leader Behaviors to Identify Knowledge Gaps

- *Review actual results versus expectations.*
- *Observe behavior versus expectations.*
- *Ask questions about results and behavior. Be curious.*
- *Listen to the answers completely before follow-up.*
- *Avoid blaming. Keep focused on identifying the gap.*
- *Ask confirming questions to determine the gap.*

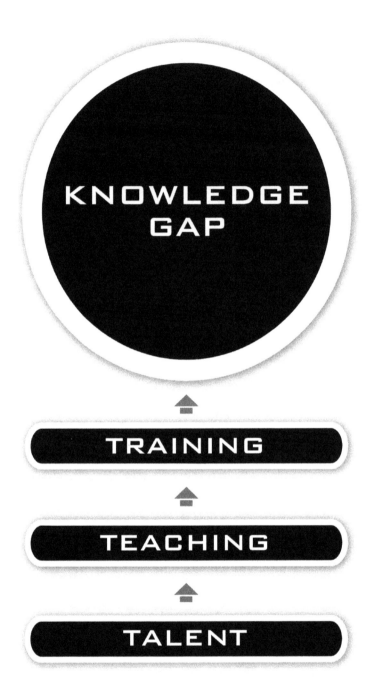

2

CLOSING
KNOWLEDGE GAPS

Closing Knowledge Gaps looks simple.

Just tell the team what they need to know, right? Just send an email or hold a meeting, and there will be no gaps, right?

Not so quick. Some leaders create more gaps than they close! Winning leaders verify Knowledge Gaps are closed, and when gaps do occur, they look for their personal gaps first. Knowledge Gaps most often originate with the leader, so it is up to the leader to close them.

"Knowledge Gaps most often originate with the leader."

By closing their own Performance Gaps, winning leaders close gaps in the team. Contrast that behavior with the C-Group, which tends to cast blame for gaps to the team. And that is why they don't win. They demoralize the team, and they are not focused on the correct Root Solutions. Blame serves no purpose. Identify and close the gaps.

As you learned in the previous chapter, Maddy is as much to blame for the miss in achieving the sales plan in period one as her team. Many leaders want their personal gaps swept under the rug, but gaps that go unidentified or get hidden away do not get closed. Remember that identifying and closing gaps quickly and permanently is a leader's role.

Winning leaders know that their personal behavior matters, and when a team is not performing, they look at their own behavior first. The gaps in the leader's behavior should be the highest priority because they create gaps in the team.

When your team is not performing to your expectations, start by looking in the mirror. What are your Performance Gaps?

Maddy worked to close the Knowledge Gaps identified in an urgent meeting the following day. She had the three-step selling process presented to the team by one of the sales managers who was instrumental in its development and who also exceeded the sales plan by the most for the period. Peer presentations from those who are performing well are a great Knowledge Gap closing tactic. It adds credibility to the message, and in this case it closes Knowledge Gaps around the three-step process.

The team asked some very good questions during the presentation, and now it appeared that all ten sales managers understood the three-step process! Although overdue, this was a big first step in closing this Knowledge Gap!

Maddy verified that the four sales managers who did not execute the three-step process now had a complete understanding by calling on each of them individually, asking for their understanding of the commitment, and asking for any additional questions. Maddy closed the meeting assuming that her team would execute the process in period two and achieve the sales plan.

Knowledge Gaps closed?

Yes and no. In this case the Knowledge Gaps are most likely closed with the sales manager team, but as you will see, closing the Knowledge Gaps does not always ensure performance will happen. Knowledge Gaps are the first gaps that need to be closed, but closing them does not mean the Importance and Action Gaps are closed. Closing the Knowledge Gap alone does not equal winning. A winning performance is achieved when the all gaps are closed.

As you will soon see, because of her assumption that the team will achieve the sales plan for period two; Maddy remains vulnerable to more Performance Gaps.

We discovered six behaviors winning leaders use to close Knowledge Gaps. Maddy will need to use all six of these to get sales on track for period two.

Winning Leader Behaviors to Close Knowledge Gaps

- *Declare the Knowledge Gaps.*
- *Seek feedback on the declaration.*
- *Ask for solutions and accept blame.*
- *Gain commitment to the solutions offered.*
- *Set expectations.*
- *Follow up and verify the commitment*

GAPOLOGY LESSONS
CLOSING KNOWLEDGE GAPS

Closing Knowledge Gaps looks simple.

Winning leaders verify Knowledge Gaps are closed, and when gaps do occur, they look for their personal gaps first. Knowledge Gaps most often originate with the leader, so it is up to the leader to close them.

Winning leaders know that their personal behavior matters, and when a team is not performing, they look at their own behavior first. The gaps in the leader's behavior should be the highest priority because they create gaps in the team.

When your team is not performing to your expectations, start by looking in the mirror.

Closing the Knowledge Gap alone does not equal winning. A winning performance is achieved when the all gaps are closed.

There are six winning leader behaviors utilized to close Knowledge Gaps:

Winning Leader Behaviors To Close Knowledge Gaps

- *Declare the Knowledge Gaps.*
- *Seek feedback on the declaration.*
- *Ask for solutions and accept blame.*
- *Gain commitment to the solutions offered.*
- *Set expectations.*
- *Follow up and verify the commitment.*

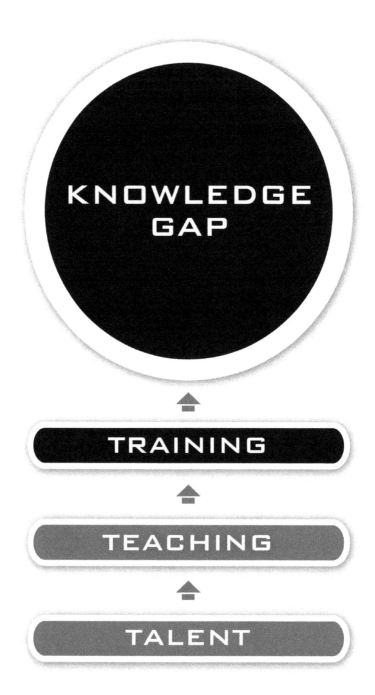

KNOWLEDGE GAP

↑

TRAINING

↑

TEACHING

↑

TALENT

44

3

TRAINING
ROOT SOLUTION

The first step to take when Knowledge Gaps are identified is to determine if there is a training issue.

Many leaders overestimate the effectiveness and retention of training. Training often leaves Knowledge Gaps because many times training is delivered in a one-dimensional format, just focusing on providing knowledge and not on building skills and commitment to the point where the performance becomes a habit. Training needs to be much more than mere communication of material. The trainer may create the gap by assuming that the team member has developed the skills and has the commitment to consistently perform to the expected level.

"Most training never gets to the Habit Level."

Assumption without verification creates a gap.

Just giving people information doesn't mean that they have the skill and desire to do it. Remember this quote: "Telling ain't training!"

Anticipate Knowledge Gaps. We estimate that 50 percent retention of the knowledge gained during training is very optimistic. For the training of a task or process to have been effective, it has to be practiced to the point of becoming habit. Habit, in this case, means a repeatable skill. Most training never reaches the level of habit. This is a significant source of Performance Gaps!

HABIT LADDER

We recommend the use of a simple ladder to gauge the point of retention of a trainee during the training process. The following flow works for most training situations and is what we call the Habit Ladder, Figure 8. Moving training to the Habit Level should be the objective of the training of a task or process.

Let's use Maddy's sales rep team (the level below the sales managers) and the new three-step selling process as the examples to explain the Habit Ladder. Starting at the bottom of the ladder and working to the top it goes like this:

COMMUNICATION

My sales manager has told me about the three-step process.

UNDERSTANDING

I have had my questions answered, and I understand the three-step process in theory.

AGREEMENT

I agree to use the three-step process with all of my customers, and I understand what is expected of me. I am committed to the process.

PRACTICE

I have role-played the three-step process with my sales manager and peers and have shown the ability to effectively execute all three steps with customers.

HABIT

I use the three-step process with every customer and have experienced the success that comes from the three steps. I am an expert, committed to the process, and an advocate to my peers.

FIGURE 8 - HABIT LADDER

Some questions for leaders to consider:

Does your training for new hires and rollouts of new procedures bring the train-ees to the Habit Level? Our experience is that most training comes up short and often only rises to the Understanding Level.

Do meetings you conduct bring the team above the Agreement Level? Do you even pursue agreement? How can you change the meeting structure to achieve this? Our experience is that most meetings do not consider the Habit Ladder when being planned or executed, and then down the road the meeting effective-ness is questioned.

Do you see how incorrect assumptions made about the effectiveness of training leave open the possibility for significant Performance Gaps? What are some ways to use the Habit Ladder to reduce gaps? Can you develop a plan to achieve each step on the ladder and a measure to know you are there?

Where do winning leaders ensure their training climbs to on the ladder? Yes, Habit Level is a key to winning behavior because that turns training into action.

As you will read in the Maddy's Story at the end of this chapter, the Habit Lad-der becomes Maddy's secret weapon in driving the three-step selling process to improve execution and close Performance Gaps. Use it!

If you assume that Knowledge Gaps are the result of training issues, retrain. But where a process or task is involved, be sure to retrain to the Habit Level. Only then will you close the gaps. If gaps recur, you will know the root cause is some-thing else.

Recurring Knowledge Gaps by the same team member suggest that you have the wrong person in the role. Retraining can be a trap that hides the real issue. No amount of training can really overcome the wrong person in the role, so make the tough decision. Therefore, Training as a Root Solution to closing Knowledge Gaps has its limitations.

HOW ADULTS LEARN

One of the most misunderstood and least considered factors in training is that people learn differently, specifically adults. If the design of your training is "one size fits all," you are likely creating Performance Gaps.

You may have heard the old saying, "You can't teach an old dog new tricks." This is true, unless you know how the old dog learns.

This saying is certainly something to consider if you are a leader who hires adults entering the workforce or changing careers, regardless of their age. Most training does not take into account that adults learn differently. This gap in training can cause adult learning retention to be lower, causing Performance Gaps.

We boil adult learning down to four simple rules that we've found winning leaders consistently leverage in their workplace. Most adults are unique in that they come with experiential knowledge gathered from years of life and workplace experience. This can be either good or bad, but in any case these years of learning need to be considered to effectively prevent Knowledge Gaps.

FOUR KEY RULES OF ADULT LEARNING:

- Adults learn when they feel the need to learn and the content is relevant to them personally.

- Adults learn best when their unique experiences are considered.

- Adults learn best and retain more when a variety of instructional approaches and contexts are used.

- Adults need practice and feedback until successful in a behavior.

Do you design your training with these things in mind? How about your meetings and conference calls? Can you see how these rules can have a positive impact on the learning and retention of adults? If you are like many leaders, you may have some work to do here. This potential gap in training can create an unreal perception of its effectiveness.

Have you ever said, "But we covered that in the meeting! How could they have missed it?"

By applying these four key rules and using the Habit Ladder, we have found that meetings, conference calls, and training are dramatically more effective and more fun!

Winning leaders seem to instinctively understand and leverage these four rules of adult learning to create winning teams.

Here are some of the tactics we learned from winning leaders that you can also use to leverage the four key rules in your meetings and training:

- Give adults the business case for the learning. Tell them why it is critical and what it will do for them. Make the learning nonnegotiable and set expectations. Lead off with this tactic.

- Ask them to design or have input on their own training agenda, and have them develop a list of topics they feel they will need more or less of. Get their input into the agenda of a meeting or conference call.

- Design meetings with a variety of delivery media: group discussion; visual, individual, and group work sessions; and pre-work and post-meeting assignments. Measure the outcomes of training and meetings with testing and feedback surveys.

- Create hands-on training where possible and provide feedback. Assign mentors for ongoing feedback and follow-up.

Meetings and conference calls have an inherent ineffectiveness that can be a source of considerable frustration for leaders. Have you ever conducted a call only to find out that little of the content was retained and turned into action? We certainly have had that experience. Many leaders do not know how adults learn and retain information. Because of this, they tend to conduct meetings and calls that are no more than boring downloads of information.

Here are some more tips we learned from winning leaders to make meetings and conference calls sources of action by applying the adult learning rules:

- Send an agenda and where applicable require preparation.

- Include guest speakers who come to share success stories on the topic to be covered. When possible, use a guest speaker who is a peer of the group attending the call or meeting. This heightens engagement and makes it real, instead of just the boss talking again.

- Ask for random recaps during the call or meeting. For example, "John, can you give us the key takeaways from what we just discussed?" Become known for this and do it frequently, and your attendees will be engaged like never before. They do not want to be embarrassed by not knowing.

- When participation is lacking, ask attendees by name to answer questions or discuss how they are executing a specific activity.

- End each call or meeting with a group discussion on key actions as an outcome. As before, choose those not participating. The group recap of key actions is a good indicator for you to know who got it and who did not. You can use the recap as an excellent predictor of where Performance Gaps will appear.

- Set clear expectations of the actions resulting from the call or meeting. Gain the group's commitment to those actions.

WINNING COMPANIES MINIMIZE KNOWLEDGE GAPS WITH THEIR CUSTOMERS

Great performance means minimizing the Knowledge Gaps not only with your team, but with your customers, too. Winning companies have figured this out and can be a source of learning for all leaders. We have three simple examples to share. All three, likely without knowing it, use Gapology to ensure there are no Knowledge Gaps with their customers.

Our first example is also one of our favorite stops, In-N-Out Burger, the legendary fast food drive-thru restaurant based in Southern California. They are famous for great burgers, fries, and shakes, but are also known for the highest quality of service in the fast food industry. Since each burger is cooked to order, the possibilities for disappointment by having Knowledge Gaps with the customer are very high. McDonald's and other fast food restaurants work around this possibility by preparing your burger in advance, so this is a key differentiator for In-N-Out.

To excel with this unique service model, In-N-Out executes what we call a "triple-check" process. Let's walk through the steps and look at their robust drive-thru execution. The drive-thru represents the majority of their business in most locations.

- As you pull up to the speaker, you are greeted with, "How's it going? What can I make for you today?"

- After you have stated your order, it is repeated back, "So I've got a number one, cooked well done, with mustard and onions only, fries, and a strawberry shake. Is that right?"

- After confirming, you drive to the first window to pay, where your order is repeated a second time.

- After confirming and paying, it is on to the pick-up window, where your order is repeated once again as you anxiously anticipate its arrival.

This "triple-check" process has served them well, and as you know if you've eaten there, they rarely get an order wrong. There is something about having a burger made to order your way that closes a Knowledge Gap with the customer to begin with.

When the Gapology team members get off the plane in California, we immediately seek out and find the nearest In-N-Out.

Our second example is Home Depot, the dominant force in the "do it yourself" home improvement business. As stated, the most obvious Root Solution starting point for an identified Knowledge Gap is training, but with many of today's tight or nonexistent training budgets, is that always realistic? Can you simply train team members with the knowledge needed to sell and service home improvement customers? The answer is "no." Imagine buying plumbing supplies from a team member that has not installed plumbing. The whole idea of "do it yourself" goes out the window, if you are relying on help from a non-expert.

Home Depot, a winning company, has figured out how to minimize Knowledge Gaps in their team members that would get passed on to customers, without just applying training. Home Depot hires their best customers, who come with years of contractor or handyman expertise. They also bring a passion for "do it yourself" that is contagious, getting passed on to customers.

Home Depot closes Knowledge Gaps with their customers by hiring product experts and "do it yourself" generalist experts to sell product to their customers. This strategy works. They supplement this expertise with training, but don't rely on training alone. They also are continuing to expand their "do it for me" business, providing experts to perform the service or installation. This model works, and their business is very strong.

Our third example and a favorite daily stop for the Gapology team is Starbucks Coffee.

Starbucks has a different challenge. The frequency of drinking a Starbucks means there is no margin for error without damaging the brand. This execution model, which must be virtually perfect, has to be accomplished in an environment that may have high employee turnover and therefore many new team members. In spite of this, Starbucks executes at a world-class level.

Obviously, there is no substitute for training when it comes to making your morning cappuccino. Starbucks baristas receive forty hours of training before they make that cup of coffee for you. Starbucks's model of an extremely high customer visit frequency means that perfection of product consistency is vital. Knowledge Gaps are overcome by writing down the order directly on the cup, and repeating the details back to the customer, whether at the counter or drive-thru. This is the key to the consistency that Starbucks achieves

You know exactly what you want, and you expect it the same way you had it yesterday. That means the same temperature, flavor, smoothness, etc. So they train, train, and retrain.

Starbucks goes a step further, empowering their teams to delight the customer in different ways than just perfection in product delivery. Here is an example: One of our friends, Susan, drives out of her way each morning to go to the same Starbucks. She literally drives by one Starbucks and a few other local coffee chains to get to "her" Starbucks. When asked why she would go out of her way, she said, "Because they make my day! Come with me."

So, we got in her car and drove about fifteen minutes to "her" Starbucks. When we pulled up to the drive-thru microphone, the barista on the other end said, and "Good morning, Susan! Do you want anything to go with your double cappuccino?" That was impressive. Then, when we pulled up to the window, the barista took the money, gave Susan her drink, and said, "Have a great day, Susan!"

As we drove off, Susan said, "See?" She held up her cup, and written on it were the words, "HAVE A GREAT DAY, SUSAN!" Susan drives out of her way to a Starbucks that makes her day. They have gained knowledge of what Susan wants, and they use it to solidify their relationship with her. Susan thrives on the personal touch and the double cappuccino. Knowledge Gap closed!

Personalized service closes the Knowledge Gap with the customer, and winning companies have figured that out. Within winning companies, winning leaders have been empowered to make great decisions, like this Starbucks manager. The bottom line is that winning leaders find out what their customers want and then they give it to them. Repeat business is the key to business today. There is no surplus of new customers, so retention is key.

Every company must deal with Knowledge Gaps. In-N-Out Burger, Home Depot, and Starbucks overcome them in different ways, and we can learn from their experience. Step back and examine your team, company, or organization and see what "macro" Knowledge Gaps may exist with your customers. Have you clearly addressed what the customer wants and needs? Have you identified products and services that your customer may not even know they would want and grow to need? Once they are identified, develop processes to execute and close these gaps. That is Gapology!

MADDY'S STORY
THE HABIT LADDER

You may not see it yet, but I will let you in on a secret. The Habit Ladder aligns with the Gapology model. Because of this, you can measure the closure of gaps using the Habit Ladder.

The Communication and Understanding steps measure the closure of the Knowledge Gap. Communication alone does not close the Knowledge Gap. Until you achieve the Understanding Level, you have not closed the Knowledge Gap. Think of these in the context of a trainer teaching a new process to a team. Understanding of the material must be measured to know if the training was effective in communicating the process. This still does not, however, ensure the new process will be implemented correctly.

The Agreement Level measures the Importance Gap. Being in agreement and committing to execute this new process ensures the Importance Gap is closed. Most training never gets this far, stopping either at Communication or Understanding. You can ask for agreement and commitment. One tactic I have used here is to ask the trainees what agreement looks like in relation to the training. This closes the Importance Gap quickly, especially if their leader is in the session. I often ask the group and then individuals, "Are you in?" Their answers let you know if the Agreement Level has been achieved.

The Practice and Habit Levels measure the Action Gap. These steps bring the training to life and make it sustainable. They also convert the training into action, performance, and ultimately results.

Once I learned this, I ensured my team used the Habit Ladder to design and measure all training--most importantly, to measure the level of each trainee.

First, we designed all training to achieve Habit Level. This alone was revolutionary! Most training targets the Understanding Level, assuming that the training will be taken to action. By forcing training to include a plan to achieve Habit Level, the training plan became much more comprehensive.

Then we started to measure all trainees. Picture a poster of the Habit Ladder and sticky dots with the names of the trainees placed at the level they achieve. Their leader can do this, or in some training classes we had the trainees place their own sticky dot on the poster and explain why. This is a great way to close a meeting, and it creates a commitment that is hard to replicate.

The Habit Ladder has become my personal secret weapon. I share it with everyone, except the competition. It gives me an edge that is hard to beat by turning training into action, performance, and results.

MADDY'S LEARNINGS

Use the Habit Ladder to design and to measure training and the rollouts of new processes or programs.

Teach the trainers and other leaders that the Habit Ladder is the measurement tool of the effectiveness of the training or the rollout. Expect a plan for all training planned for delivery to include information on how they will achieve a Habit Level rollout.

Blow up the Habit Ladder to poster size and put people's names on it, showing the level they have achieved. The same tactic can be used for training or new processes. Place them on the poster. If you are rolling out five new processes this year, where does each of them stand on the Habit Ladder? Make Habit Level the target for all training and all trainees.

GAPOLOGY LESSONS
TRAINING
ROOT SOLUTION

The first step to take when Knowledge Gaps are identified is to determine if there is a training issue.

Many leaders overestimate the effectiveness and retention of training. Training often leaves Knowledge Gaps because many times training is delivered in a one-dimensional format, just focusing on providing knowledge and not on building skills and commitment to the point where the performance becomes a habit. Training needs to be much more than mere communication of material. The trainer may create the gap by assuming that the team member has developed the skills and has the commitment to consistently perform to the expected level.

Just giving someone the information doesn't mean that they have the skill and desire to use it. Remember this quote: "Telling ain't training!"

We recommend the use of a simple ladder to gauge the point of retention of a trainee during the training process. The following flow works for most training situations and is what we call the Habit Ladder. Moving training to the Habit Level should be the objective of the training of a task or process.

COMMUNICATION

My sales manager has told me about the three-step process.

UNDERSTANDING

I have had my questions answered, and I understand the three-step process in theory.

AGREEMENT

I agree to use the three-step process with all of my customers, and I understand what is expected of me. I am committed to the process.

PRACTICE

I have role-played the three-step process with my sales manager and peers and have shown the ability to effectively execute all three steps with customers.

HABIT

I use the three-step process with every customer and have experienced the success that comes from the three steps. I am an expert, committed to the process, and an advocate to my peers.

If you assume that Knowledge Gaps are the result of training issues, retrain. But where a process or task is involved, be sure to retrain to the Habit Level. Only then will you close the gaps. If gaps recur, you will know the root cause is something else.

Recurring Knowledge Gaps by the same team member suggest that you have the wrong person in the role. Retraining can be a trap that hides the real issue.

One of the most misunderstood and least considered factors in training is that people learn differently, specifically adults. If the design of your training is "one size fits all," you are likely creating Performance Gaps.

FOUR KEY RULES OF ADULT LEARNING

- Adults learn when they feel the need to learn and the content is relevant to them personally.
- Adults learn best when their unique experiences are considered.
- Adults learn best and retain more when a variety of instructional approaches and contexts are used.
- Adults need practice and feedback until successful in a behavior.

Here are some of the tactics we learned from winning leaders that you can also use to leverage the four key rules in your meetings and training:

- Give adults the business case for the learning. Tell them why it is critical and what it will do for them. Make the learning nonnegotiable and set expectations. Lead off with this tactic.
- Ask them to design or have input on their own training agenda, and have them develop a list of topics they feel they will need more or less of. Get their input regarding the agenda of a meeting or conference call
- Design meetings with a variety of delivery media: group discussion; visual, individual, and group work sessions; and pre-work and post-meeting assignments. Measure the outcomes of training and meetings with testing and feedback surveys.
- Create hands-on training where possible and provide feedback. Assign mentors for ongoing feedback and follow up.

Great performance means minimizing the Knowledge Gaps not only with your team, but with your customers, too. Winning companies have figured this out and can be a source of learning for all leaders.

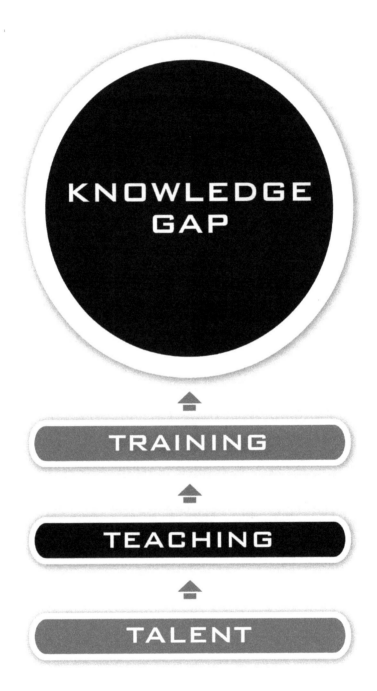

4

TEACHING
ROOT SOLUTION

One of the keys to closing ongoing Knowledge Gaps is for leaders to perform a teaching role.

In our research, leaders in the C-Group exclusively overlook this strategy. They tend to "tell" or "command" but not teach. We consider this a common thread in their poor performance.

Winning leaders know that is key to achieving organizational wisdom.. They develop and deliver "Teachable Points of View," or TPOVs for short, to their teams, remaining in the teaching mode at all times. They carve teaching into their daily rhythm, using teaching in short bursts to create learning and close Knowledge Gaps in their teams.

"Winning leaders know that teaching is key to achieving organizational wisdom."

TPOVs TAKE ON VARIOUS FORMS:

- Stump Speech

- Creating a Shared Vision

- Making the Business Case

- New Process Demonstration

- Selling Change

STUMP SPEECH

Like a politician running for office, winning leaders are always ready to speak to groups of team members and other leaders at any time. One way to be prepared is to have a current living "stump speech." The stump speech may be focused around the organization's mission, business plan, or key expectations. It should be limited to just a few memorable minutes. You may want to take notes on index cards until you gain comfort with the delivery.

We recommend the use of a stump speech to talk about your expectations, delivering the same consistent message whenever you are with leaders and team members. Present the message in a format that can easily be remembered by the team and repeated by others. A stump speech can be used in person or on conference calls. When possible, leave time for questions, ensuring understanding and fulfilling the purpose of teaching.

A stump speech delivered by leaders is one key to keeping Knowledge Gaps closed around what you are trying to accomplish as a team. A compelling stump speech will spread to others, who will deliver the message in their own words.

We have found that winning leaders were prepared and comfortable with delivering compelling stump speeches without notice, and they set an expectation for other leaders within their team to be able to do the same.

The spontaneity of a stump speech brings with it a credibility that is hard to replicate with another medium.

CREATING A SHARED VISION

Similar to the stump speech, having prepared talking points around their vision was a key tactic used by winning leaders for closing any potential Knowledge Gaps. They share what they believe in and where the organization is going, using this vision to create devoted followers. The talking points are used most often face-to-face or in small groups.

This method is about bringing others along on a journey to somewhere compelling, and it is a very high bar for any leader. Be prepared for two-way dialogue and questions. Creating a "shared vision" isn't easy, and you will need to be compelling and motivating if you are going to create something big that others will believe in.

To sharpen your skill, we suggest you rehearse your delivery in front of a mirror or on video. Unlike a stump speech, don't use index cards. This one has got to come from the heart to be effective. After all, you are trying to make your vision their vision.

MAKING THE BUSINESS CASE

Leaders are often asked to explain why the organization has made a decision to move in a strategic direction or implement a significant change. Leaders need to be prepared to explain why the decision was made in a format that will allow other leaders to deliver that same explanation to their teams.

One tactic is to hand out or send a digital copy of your talking points of the business case after spoken delivery. This ensures that team members will have the correct details and allows them to advocate your points with others. In live sessions, set aside time for questions and answers, too. There is no room for Knowledge Gaps when explaining the business case.

The execution of any significant change is only as good as the leader's ability to explain it.

Winning leaders are great at making the business case for change. While change derails some leaders and organizations, winning leaders and organizations make it look seamless. They know the importance of being able to remain nimble and able to change.

NEW PROCESS DEMONSTRATION

Leaders should understand and be prepared to explain and demonstrate new processes. It is very powerful for the leader to have more than just a high level of knowledge of a process, even if he or she is not the one performing it on a daily basis. This shows the leader's engagement and buy-in to the process, which is rare today.

For example, Starbucks's store managers and district managers are trained baristas and know how to make every coffee drink. This is a Knowledge Gap game changer! What a powerful way to support the brand and create a culture of consistency!

Imagine the Knowledge Gaps that are exposed when the leadership knows the processes firsthand. Leaders who insulate themselves from the process and act as if it is not their job to know it will rarely achieve greatness.

Winning leaders stay close to new or changing processes to ensure there are minimal Performance Gaps.

SELLING THE CHANGE

During times of change, leadership is the lighthouse in the fog of uncertainty. Winning leaders navigate the treacherous waters just fine, while the rest clearly struggle. Leaders need to devote extra time each day to "sell" the change. They must prepare themselves for an increased number of coaching conversations and questions from team members. The most important element of the change conversation is centered on what it means for the team members.

USE THESE QUESTIONS TO STRUCTURE YOUR NOTES:

- Why the change? Make the business case.

- Why do you personally embrace the change?

- How will it impact the team member? Address their number-one concern.

- What does the team member need to do now? Create a sense of urgency and a call to action.

Winning leaders excel in leading through change. This is a strength and core competency, and it really separates winning from losing and is a powerful predictor of success. It should be a key area of questioning during the interview process for prospective leaders.

If you have not developed this skill, work on it, and it will help drive performance and results. Winning leaders embrace change and know that it is the only constant. They expect it and choose to thrive, while others fight it and grow frustrated.

When leading through change and confronting direct reluctance to change, refer to the DABA Change Ladder, Figure 9 on the next page. It is a "must-have" for the toolboxes of winning leaders and will help you understand your own change resistance and coach team members through the four phases of change.

You may have seen this model in a different form, but this version is the most accurate as a coaching tool. Humans react to change very predictably and it flows as follows:

DENIAL

"This isn't happening. It will go away."

ANGER

"Why me? Why now? This won't work."

BARGAINING

"Can we do this a different way? How about a different time? Can I have input?"

ACCEPTANCE

"We can do this. What do you need from me? How can I help? What is my role? When can we start?"

Watch for these specific phases in yourself and in your team. You will discover that the anger phase is actually a good sign because it suggests that there is movement away from the denial phase.

In some people there is a wall that prevents them from moving past anger to the productive bargaining and acceptance phases. So, when coaching a team through change, be aware of the wall and be patient. Spend time listening during this phase. This allows concerns to surface, and often, discussing these concerns is what is needed to help people move to acceptance.

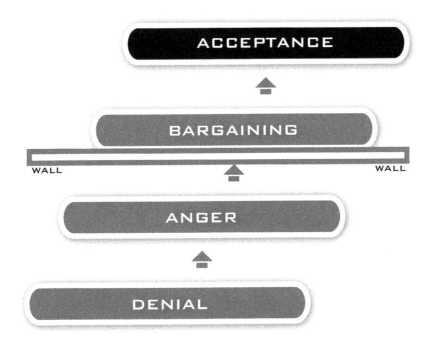

FIGURE 9 - DABA CHANGE LADDER

During any major change, winning leaders overly communicate to achieve acceptance and buy-in from their team. Use the DABA Change Ladder and observe the behavior of key team members during change to be most effective.

Leaders are the most important catalyst in a team's path to acceptance of change.

One successful tactic we have observed is to enlist those who move quickly to acceptance to mentor and partner with those who hit the wall and are stuck in denial. Sometimes a peer can help to create more movement through the DABA Change Ladder than a supervisor.

MADDY'S STORY
WINNING LEADERSHIP RHYTHM

Winning leadership rhythm is my consistent and predictable way of leading. This rhythm not only moves my team to great performance and results, but it is also a form of teaching. My team emulates my behavior and therefore my rhythm.

The purpose of my leadership rhythm is to make performance and achieving results important. My team observes everything I do and don't do. My behavior or rhythm teaches what matters, so it must match my spoken expectations. I can't say that the customer comes first, then not visit customers during my time with sales reps. Everything a leader does communicates importance to the team, and a great leadership rhythm teaches an example to others on how to behave.

Let me give you some examples of my rhythm.

Every Monday I speak to my team on a conference call. Conference calls are hardly an effective method of changing behavior, but because my team is spread across a rather significant geography, conference calls are the most effective two-way communication option. I apply my rhythm tactics to meetings as well.

So, why do I speak to my team every Monday? It is part of my continuous teaching. Additionally, my leadership rhythm drives the performance of my team. I work to close Knowledge and Importance Gaps and lead the team to action. I am very predictable. The call is very predictable in flow. That's the rhythm part. I use my leadership rhythm to make performance important and shape behavior. My team always knows the focus, what results will be reviewed, and what questions will be asked. The sales managers then take the message and

---

rhythm to the sales reps. That is the teaching part.

Here are some key tactics I use to make conference calls and meetings more effective in closing gaps and creating action:

I autopsy the previous week's sales performance and the status of the period-to-date results. This makes results important, so I choose which results I recap carefully. I know my team places importance on what I recap, so I may create Importance Gaps by discussing results that are of lesser importance. This is a common leadership mistake that can be avoided by keeping a narrow focus on the most critical results. I teach what matters through this part of the rhythm.

I remind the team of my expectations each week and how they are performing against those expectations. This keeps them focused on the big picture and creates importance around the expectations. I teach big picture here, providing context for what we discuss.

I recognize the top performers in the metrics that measure my expectations. This shapes their focus and their behavior all week leading up to the conference call. This creates an open book test each week. The team knows what is expected and what will be celebrated. I teach what we value here. With my rhythm, it helps for my team to be comprised of a competitive group of people because we have fun competing and trash talking respectfully.

The best must teach. We share everything that works. I ask the top performers to explain why they are winning, and then I have the team ask questions about their tactics. This sharing is a key to teamwork and interdependence. Peers sharing tactics add credibility to those tactics and improve execution. Teams are more likely to execute a tactic if a peer has already tried it and had success.

We set or update behavioral expectations that will deliver the results expectations for the week and period. I ask the team, "So, what are the expectations, both results and behavioral?" I let them state the expectations, and then I ask each person on the call if the expectations are clear. If not, I ask the team to clarify. This closes any potential Importance Gaps and creates sharing and interdependence.

I close the call by creating an open book test and once again clarifying the expectations for the current week. I give the answers to the test. This shapes the team's behavior for the week and closes any remaining Importance Gaps airtight.

As the weeks and periods play out, I remain narrowly focused, predictable, and intentional. I need my team narrowly focused on the execution needed to achieve the desired outcomes that are the measures of my expectations. When I visit with my team in the field, talk to them on the phone, or exchange email communication, my focus remains narrow, predictable, and intentional.

I follow my leadership rhythm, and this creates a rhythm in my team. Redundant? Yes, redundant, but intentional, with a focus on things that really matter. This is teaching what matters over and over again. Rhythm. Repetitive. Predictable.

This is a huge part of my success as a winning leader. Create a leadership rhythm of your own and stick to it.

So how do I deal with underperformance?

When a leader on my team underperforms for the period and does not meet expectations or falls to the bottom of the performance ranker as compared to the rest of the team, I require them to attend what I call a "gap" meeting.

Everyone on my team knows underperformance for the period will equal attendance at a "gap" meeting. It is also a part of my leadership rhythm and is designed to shape the team's behavior throughout the period. A "gap" meeting is an autopsy of the underperformance for the period.

Here are the things examined in the gap meeting:

Which results were missed for the period?

Which behaviors were not in place that caused the results miss?

What is the commitment to results and changed behavior for the upcoming period?

My team does not necessarily like to attend gap meetings, but that is part of the reason that they are so effective in moving performance. Gap meetings are designed to be very supportive, but can be uncomfortable because they expose opportunity areas. But that is precisely how progress is made. That is why they are part of my leadership rhythm and that of my team's rhythm as they lead their teams. They are predictable, and everyone knows who is in them. They also know that you can only attend a few gap meetings.

On my team you either close the gap or you are the gap. Performance is not optional. Everyone knows this because they hear it from me and experience it, too!

MADDY'S LESSONS

You may have heard that leaders create followers. While this is true, I prefer to say that leaders create leaders. Part of this creation process is teaching via the behavior and rhythm of a leader. This is how I pass on everything, and it is real because they see me do it. I am a teacher first, and along with that comes my leadership.

Which gaps are most impacted by leadership rhythm? The answer is that Importance Gaps and Action Gaps are the primary targets for closure. A leadership rhythm that makes the winning leader's expectations extremely important is a rhythm that moves the team to action.

A strong leadership rhythm is a top tactic of high-performance winning leaders It also creates leaders.

GAPOLOGY LESSONS
TEACHING
ROOT SOLUTION

One of the keys to closing ongoing Knowledge Gaps is for leaders to perform a teaching role.

Winning leaders know that teaching is key to achieving organizational wisdom. They develop and deliver "Teachable Points of View," or TPOVs for short, to their teams, remaining in the teaching mode at all times. They carve teaching into their daily rhythm, using teaching in short bursts to create learning and close Knowledge Gaps in their teams.

TPOVs TAKE ON VARIOUS FORMS:

- Stump Speech
- Creating a Shared Vision
- Making the Business Case
- New Process Demonstration
- Selling Change

Selling the Change

During times of change, leadership is the lighthouse in the fog of uncertainty. Winning leaders navigate the treacherous waters just fine, while the rest clearly struggle. Leaders need to devote extra time each day to "sell" the change.

USE THESE QUESTIONS TO STRUCTURE YOUR NOTES:

- Why the change? Make the business case.
- Why do you personally embrace the change?
- How will it impact the team member? Address their number-one concern.
- What does the team member need to do now? Create a sense of urgency and a call to action.

Winning leaders excel in leading through change. This is a strength and core competency, and it really separates winning from losing and is a powerful predictor of success.

When leading through change and confronting direct reluctance to change, refer to the DABA Change Ladder.

DENIAL

"This isn't happening. It will go away."

ANGER

"Why me? Why now? This won't work."

BARGAINING

"Can we do this a different way? How about a different time? Can I have input?"

ACCEPTANCE

"We can do this. What do you need from me? How can I help? What is my role? When can we start?"

Watch for these specific phases in yourself and your team. You will discover that the anger phase is actually a good sign because it suggests that there is movement away from the denial phase.

During any major change, winning leaders overly communicate to achieve acceptance and buy-in from their team. Use the DABA model and observe the behavior of key team members during change to be most effective.

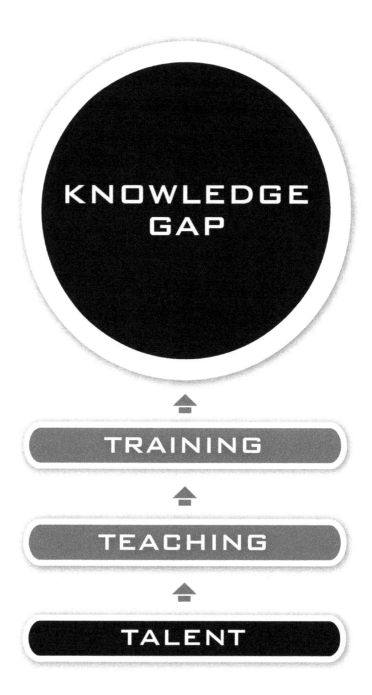

KNOWLEDGE GAP

↑

TRAINING

↑

TEACHING

↑

TALENT

5

TALENT
ROOT SOLUTION

Ultimately, the more talented and skilled the team you lead, the fewer Knowledge Gaps you will experience.

Talent matters, and putting the right person in the right role makes a huge difference in performance. This chapter makes this case from different angles, gives you insight into your team, and teaches you how to construct a winning team.

"For closing Performance Gaps, talent with the right mindset trumps everything else."

Winning leaders spend a significant amount of time hiring and developing talent. It is often their primary focus because it creates their competitive edge. They know that for closing Performance Gaps, talent with the right mindset trumps everything else. In fact, when it comes to performance, winning leaders know that talent is a key ingredient, whether they've developed talent organically or acquired it externally.

"PLAY CHESS, NOT CHECKERS"

One of the core principles of Gapology and a foundational principle of winning leaders is that performance is dependent upon getting the right person in the right role. When winning leaders make changes to the team and move people from one position or location to another, they do so very strategically.

Winning leaders' behavior when it comes to "people moves" is strategic and deliberate, thus, "Play chess, not checkers."

"Play chess" means that each people move is strategic, is thought-out, and has a purpose. It also means that leaders are planning future moves as they make each move.

The contrast with checkers is that checkers is easier and more tactical. Moves are typically made more quickly with less thought. Since people moves are generally the most important decisions leaders make, these moves must be made carefully and strategically; thus chess, not checkers.

We designed the following exercises to help you develop your winning chess strategy. We use Maddy's team as the examples.

The first step is to rank your team. Let's say you have ten direct reports, each in the same position, just like Maddy. Rank them from one to ten using the following process: one being the highest ranked, and ten being the lowest ranked.

We recommend a multidimensional team ranking process based upon three criteria: achievement of results, alignment with organizational values, and overall leadership qualities. We call this the Leadership Ranking. It gives leaders an excellent balance and keeps leaders from over ranking those who gets results the wrong way and may not live the organization's values. At the same time, it highlights those that live the values but don't get results. The Leadership Ranking also keeps the leader's eye on the future and on developing a team with strong leadership skills capable of moving to the next level.

Winning leaders know that the ideal team produces great results, is aligned with the organization's values, and has strong leadership, thus creating a bright future for the organization. Checkmate!

RESULTS		VALUES		TALENT	
Michael	1	Michael	7	Michael	4
Emma	2	Emma	2	Emma	9
Jamaal	3	Jamaal	8	Jamaal	6
Aliya	4	Aliya	6	Aliya	10
Javier	5	Javier	3	Javier	2
Sara	6	Sara	4	Sara	1
Isaac	7	Isaac	1	Isaac	7
Li	8	Li	5	Li	5
Matt	9	Matt	10	Matt	3
Lucia	10	Lucia	9	Lucia	8

AVERAGE SCORE		LEADERSHIP RANKING
Michael	4.00	3
Emma	4.33	4
Jamaal	5.67	6
Aliya	6.67	8
Javier	3.33	1
Sara	3.67	2
Isaac	5.00	5
Li	6.00	7
Matt	7.33	9
Lucia	9.00	10

Let's look at the table above of the Leadership Ranking, as well as the process Maddy uses for the team of ten sales managers.

Michael is the top results producer on the team, so he ranks number one in results. He rides the edge, though, on the organization's values and sometimes rides along an ethical line. He has been coached and has responded, but seems to go back to the same behavior at times. So in values he ranks seventh. He is certainly upwardly mobile and wants more from his career at XYZ, but he will need to make behavioral changes to get there. He participates in meetings and is respected by his peers. In leadership, she ranks him fourth.

MICHAEL'S LEADERSHIP AVERAGE SCORE

- Results   1
- Values   7
- Leadership   4
- Michael's Total =   12 divided by 3 = 4.0

After completing this process for your whole team, rank them in order from the lowest score to the highest score.

In this case, Michael ranks third on the team. As you can see, if we simply ranked by results, Michael would be number one, but that would not be the best thing for Michael or the company. He should know that if he can overcome the values issue, his career could really blossom. If he can't, he may not even have a future as district manager and may not be allowed to stay with XYZ.

Depending on your type of organization or its point of evolution, you can change the three ranking categories. Your other option is to weight the categories differently to create greater or lesser emphasis. We have weighted them equally, but if, for example, in your organization, results are more important than values and leadership at this stage, you could apply a 1.5 or 2.0 weighting to the results ranking.

VOLUME		UPSIDE		COMPLEXITY	
Michael	5	Michael	7	Michael	9
Emma	6	Emma	10	Emma	10
Jamaal	3	Jamaal	8	Jamaal	1
Aliya	4	Aliya	6	Aliya	7
Javier	1	Javier	7	Javier	6
Sara	9	Sara	2	Sara	4
Isaac	7	Isaac	1	Isaac	5
Li	8	Li	9	Li	2
Matt	2	Matt	4	Matt	3
Lucia	10	Lucia	5	Lucia	8

AVERAGE SCORE		POSITION RANK
Michael	7.00	8
Emma	8.67	10
Jamaal	4.00	2
Aliya	5.67	6
Javier	4.67	4
Sara	5.00	5
Isaac	4.33	3
Li	6.33	7
Matt	3.00	1
Lucia	7.67	9

Now let's look at the table above, an example of ranking the sales managers' geographical areas or current assignments. We call this the Position Ranking. It allows the leader to ensure they have the team in the right position when compared with the Leadership Ranking.

Maddy's ten sales managers are all in the greater Chicago area. She wants to be sure that she has the right sales manager in the right area. Play chess, not checkers, right? We have already ranked the sales managers in leadership, and now we are going to compare their Position Ranking and see if there is a gap.

For the Position Ranking, we use a different multidimensional approach based upon three criteria: sales volume, sales upside potential, and market complexity.

This ranking is effective for most sales organizations. Modify using three different criteria to fit your organizational structure.

Michael's sales market area in northwest Chicago is fifth in volume but has very little upside because it is a mature market, and he has developed most of the existing client base. So we rank sales volume a 5 and upside a 7. It has low complexity because it is a small, confined market with few prospects for new clients. Michael is maintaining relationships with existing clients and working to maximize their spending each period. Complexity ranks 9. Remember that you are ranking the highest volume, greatest upside, and most complexity with the lowest number.

MICHAEL'S POSITION AVERAGE SCORE:

- Volume   5
- Upside   7
- Complexity   9
- Michael's Area Total =   21 divided by 3 is **7.0**

LEADERSHIP RANK		POSITION RANK		COMPARISON	
Michael	3	Michael's Area	8	Michael	+5.00
Emma	4	Emma's Area	10	Emma	+6.00
Jamaal	6	Jamaal's Area	2	Jamaal	-4.00
Aliya	8	Aliya's Area	6	Aliya	-2.00
Javier	1	Javier's Area	4	Javier	+3.00
Sara	2	Sara's Area	5	Sara	+3.00
Isaac	5	Isaac's Area	3	Isaac	-2.00
Li	7	Li's Area	7	Li	0.00
Matt	9	Matt's Area	1	Matt	-8.00
Lucia	10	Lucia's Area	9	Lucia	-1.00

Now let's compare the Leadership Ranking versus the Position Ranking using the table above while looking for alignment opportunities. Michael's Leadership Ranking is 3 of 10 within his peer group, but his Position Ranking is 8 of 10: a gap of 5. In this case Michael's leadership is greater than the position he holds.

So what is the relevance of the gap? It means that Maddy is not maximizing Michael's leadership, and he can handle a higher-ranked position. This means that Maddy may be losing sales in an area with a lesser leader.

We consider a gap of 0 to 3 to be the ideal margin of error and the acceptable gap within a direct report team of 10. The larger your team is, the larger the acceptable margin of error. A worse scenario is the reverse, where the Leadership Ranking is lower than the Position Ranking.

What if Michael's position ranked a 3 and his leadership ranked an 8? That would be a gap of minus 5. In this case, Michael would likely not maximize the performance in his position and he may be substantially over his head, likely resulting in significant lost revenue due to Performance Gaps.

The goal is to align a team member's Leadership Ranking with his or her Position Ranking, ensuring that the right person is in the right role. So, the best-case scenario would be for Michael to have a position ranked 3, equal to his Leadership Ranking. Would that likely maximize sales and profits? Yes! Play chess, not checkers! With this process completed and with the Leadership and the Position Rankings in alignment, winning leaders separate themselves from the rest more than with any other single tactic of which we are aware. This means the right person is in the right role.

Winning leaders may not do it as formally as we've demonstrated, but they have established a process. Get good at this, and you are well on your way to winning!

SETTING THE BAR

Let's go back to the topic of the Leadership Ranking of your direct reports. Whether you hired them, promoted them, or inherited them, they are yours. As you bring others to your team, it is critical that you consider how they will rank within your current team. This should be part of the selection process.

Let's talk about "setting the bar" for your team. Assume that you have ten direct reports, and you have them ranked 1 to 10 in leadership, as illustrated in the table on the next page. How many of the ten currently meet your expectations? Another way to look at it is this: how many of the ten would you hire or promote into their current role today?

Let's take a look at the ABC Ranking Chart.

ABC RANKING	TEAM POSITION	TEAM MEMBER NAME	ACCEPTABILITY BAR LEVEL
A-PLAYERS	1		STAR PLAYER BAR LEVEL
A-PLAYERS	2		STAR PLAYER BAR LEVEL
A-PLAYERS	3		STAR PLAYER BAR LEVEL
B-PLAYERS	4		ACCEPTABLE PLAYER BAR LEVEL
B-PLAYERS	5		ACCEPTABLE PLAYER BAR LEVEL
B-PLAYERS	6		ACCEPTABLE PLAYER BAR LEVEL
C-PLAYERS	7		UNACCEPTABLE PLAYER BAR LEVEL
C-PLAYERS	8		UNACCEPTABLE PLAYER BAR LEVEL
C-PLAYERS	9		UNACCEPTABLE PLAYER BAR LEVEL
C-PLAYERS	10		UNACCEPTABLE PLAYER BAR LEVEL

Insert a bar (horizontal line) across your ranking at the level that splits the group between those meeting your expectations (above the bar) and those not meeting your expectations (below the bar). We have set this bar above between 6 and 7. This means that the direct reports in positions 7 to 10 do not meet your expectations. Knowing what you know today, you would not hire or promote these direct reports into their current role.

This is a big admission. How is their performance impacting your overall results? Are these four direct reports, 7 to 10, aware that they do not meet your expectations, and are they working to change that? Is there a plan with actions and dates?

As you hire external talent to join your direct report team, your objective must be to bring in those that will rank in the upper third of the ranking. Why hire externally if not for top talent? Then, your internal promotions must be in the upper half, at least 6 or above. This process will automatically upgrade your team each time someone is added.

We have inserted another horizontal bar to define the external hiring mark and to define the star players on the team. Those above this bar must exceed your expectations. Let's say that you have three star players, ranked 1 through 3. We now have a bar between 3 and 4 and a bar between 6 and 7.

Now your team is divided into thirds; we call these the A-Players, who are your stars, the B-Players in the middle, and the C-Players who are underperforming. This gives you a bar for external hires, 3 and above, and internal promotions, 6 and above. This should provide clarity around the actions you need to take with your team.

To move performance forward, we recommend two tactics:

- Keep the top third always moving higher. This challenges the performance of the entire team to move higher and resets the bar for the middle. The middle dreams of being the top group and then will look up to that bar to measure their own performance.

- Keep the bottom third moving up or out. If out, replace them with players who reside from day one in the middle or top third. This means that changes to the team line-up will automatically upgrade the entire team. Never fill a position just to fill a position. Be strategic and consider your forced ranking. Play chess, not checkers!

Keep your team ranked into three categories:

- A-Players are those who exceed result expectations while adhering to company values and have strong leadership.

- B-Players are those who achieve result expectations and adhere to the company values.

- C-Players are those who do not meet result expectations and may have issues with values and leadership.

Where do most leaders spend the bulk of their time? Yes, with the C-Players. This leaves the A-Players feeling undervalued and likely leaves them underdeveloped. Too often leaders believe that the A-Players need less attention and have less room to grow. Winning leaders suggest that this is totally false and that A-Players have the most room to grow. Winning leaders spend more personalized time with A-Players than any other group, followed by C-Players, then B Players.

We have found that leaders who are not meeting expectations tend to avoid hiring or promoting A-Players because they feel intimidated or threatened by them. If you fit this description, work to overcome this feeling by leveraging the A-Players. They can be great sources of learning and motivation.

Winning leaders share a philosophy of replacement leadership. They are always developing their replacement. They view it as their duty to the organization, but also as a way to strengthen and challenge the team in new directions.

Here is a recap of what we have learned from winning leaders, and we suggest taking the following approach in your leadership of your team.

- Give A-Players most of your time. They are the future of the organization. They can accomplish things that may change the trajectory of the organization. They raise the bar for the whole team and cause others, especially other A-Players and the B-Players, to step up their game. They may be your replacement when you get promoted and therefore should be a source of learning and development for you. Embrace them. Keep the A-Players involved in special projects and testing new ideas. This increases their exposure to others in the organization and drives their engagement level higher. A-Players are the most mismanaged group. They expect more from their leader and will not likely work for a B-Leader for long. They are hungry and are the highest-risk group to leave the organization.

- A-Leaders attract A-Players. A-Players want to work for A-Leaders, while C-Leaders attract and find comfort in surrounding themselves with C-Players.

- Give C-Players the second most attention. The designation of C needs to be temporary. They either improve to B or A, or they are off the team. Your time with them should be in a directive mode and accompanied with strong follow up. They lower the game of the entire team, and if you keep C-Players, it is a reflection on your leadership.

- But, don't forget that C-Players may be A-Players in disguise. Perhaps surprisingly, we have found more A-Players hiding in the "C-Weeds" than in the "B-Weeds." Look for them. Remember, Albert Einstein was a poor student. Abraham Lincoln was considered an underachiever much of his adult life. They were A-Players, but their greatness was invisible to most, or they were in the wrong role. Winning leaders can see the potential of an individual and sometimes provide the guidance to change his or her performance dramatically. That being said, many C-Players choose to be C-Players and like it there.

- B-Players don't typically need as much of your individual time, but don't ignore them. Because they make up the largest percentage of your team and deliver the largest portion of your overall results, utilize your A-Players to help grow their talent levels. The A-Players will likely thrive with this level of empowerment and the B-Players will get an opportunity to learn from their best performing peers. This helps to create buy-in for the training or coaching. The B-Players are usually the most stable performing group and are less likely to be recruited away, but they may quit on their own if they don't feel valued. They do their jobs, and your personal time with them is less likely to produce as extraordinary a result as it would spending dedicated time with the A-Players, getting that group ready to help mentor the others.

MANAGING PEOPLE UNEQUALLY

Winning leaders manage people unequally. They believe that leadership is not "one size fits all" and that it is more complex because what works to lead each team member may be different.

As we have already covered, there are A, B and C-Players on most teams. They are unique individuals, and the leader's way of leading them impacts their performance.

Winning leaders take the time to find out what works for each individual while finding their hot buttons and pushing them. They find out their needs and their wishes and provide them. Winning leaders partner with their team members to maximize their engagement and performance. This does not mean that they drop their values or compromise their leadership style, but it does mean that they have learned that effective leadership requires true situational leadership and style.

Other leaders may make the mistake of developing a style and expecting everyone to adapt to it. Winning leaders adapt to the circumstance and the players who are working to maximize the performance of each team member. People are unique, and to lead them you must manage them unequally.

TALENT CREATES TALENT

Talent creates talent, and with talent comes fewer Performance Gaps.

I cherish the day I hired Sara. She was a top talent, recruited from our top competitor. During her training, we learned more from her than we taught. Once she was in position, her team quickly moved into the top third of the Performance Rankings, and within three months she was the top performer in the entire company. I loved her performance, of course, but I loved her ability to create and attract talent even more. Talent, absolutely, creates talent!

Isaac was already on Sara's team when she joined the company. Isaac was a mediocre sales rep at best. He never even thought about being a top performer. That was not his league. He was a C-Player who did just enough to get by. He would jump up to B-Behavior long enough to get the boss off his back, and then he would drift back to C-Behavior once again. Isaac had been satisfied with living his life in the lower middle of the pack, but now that he worked for Sara he had a big problem. Sara had only one standard, and C was not it.

On her first visit with Isaac and his customers, Sara set very clear, but very high expectations. Sara knew that Isaac was the most knowledgeable member of her team, but he chose not to translate that knowledge into performance. He had the potential. She explained to Isaac that if he chose to perform to his lower standard, it meant he would need to work somewhere else. Sara had closed any Knowledge or Importance Gaps as it related to her expectations of Isaac. It was a tough few days.

Isaac thought about turning in his resignation right then, but he did not. He had outlasted his previous three supervisors and thought he would do so again...although this one seemed different.

He later confided that he had talked with his wife about resigning because of Sara and whether he could achieve her standards. She asked him, "Why resign because of Sara? So, what is wrong with Sara anyway? Is it just that she has high standards? Why don't you just raise yours? That would be a lot easier than finding a new job. You're better than this, Isaac. Quit whining and step it up!"

Isaac hated to admit it, but she was right.

He couldn't sleep that night. At around 3:00 a.m., he got up and started making notes on what he needed to change. That morning he called Sara and declared his new expectations. He set his expectations above Sara's level. Sara accepted his expectations.

Sara was shocked by the intensity of the "new" Isaac, but she was inspired by his newly found edge and strong point of view around performance. Isaac's peer group heard about the new Isaac, causing many to reflect on their own performance and personal expectations.

Isaac had moved his game from C-Player to A-Player in one sleepless night. He already had the skills to be a top performer, but he somehow lacked the motivation that Sara was able to provide.

As Sara moved to a top performer within XYZ, Isaac was right there with her. He became the top-ranked rep on Sara's team. Isaac was now an A-Player. He taught and mentored the other reps. Sara learned to rely on Isaac for his experience and strong point of view about achieving greatness. Isaac found that winning was not only fun, but also addictive. Winning is better than whining!

Isaac's impact on Sara's team of reps was nothing short of amazing. They really stepped it up. Isaac's move was the catalyst. Within a year, Isaac was promoted to district manager on Maddy's team, where he continued to be an A-Player. Talent creates talent.

Now, I said that Isaac was the catalyst for the team stepping up, but what was the catalyst for Isaac stepping up? Sara. She saw something and stuck with it. This not only strengthened her team, but also added a strong district manager to Maddy's team. A-Players create A-Players!

I cherish the day I hired Sara. Sara's anniversary date with the company is marked on my calendar, and I celebrate that day as if it were my birthday!

MADDY'S LEARNINGS

Hiring talent is the one thing that changes everything. Talented winning leaders create an environment where C-Players have the ability to transform into A-Players. A-Players are so influential that other A-Players will follow them to other companies because the experience and the synergy that they create are rare and hard to find. Beware of the C-Players, however; most will remain C-Players if given a choice. It's easier. Don't give them a choice. C-Players will recruit and tolerate C-Players on their team. A-Players excel in performance by avoiding and closing gaps.

GAPOLOGY LESSONS
TALENT
ROOT SOLUTION

Ultimately, the more talented and skilled the team you lead, the fewer Knowledge Gaps you will experience.

Talent matters, and putting the right person in the right role makes a huge difference in performance.

Winning leaders spend a significant amount of time hiring and developing talent. It is often their primary focus because it creates their competitive edge. They know that for closing Performance Gaps, talent with the right mindset trumps everything else. In fact, when it comes to performance, winning leaders know that talent is a key ingredient, whether they've developed talent organically or acquired it externally.

Winning leaders' behavior when it comes to "people moves" is strategic and deliberate, thus, "Play chess, not checkers."

"Play chess" means that each people move is strategic, is thought-out, and has a purpose. It also means that leaders are planning future moves as they make each move.

The contrast with checkers is that checkers is easier and more tactical. Moves are typically made more quickly with less thought. Since people moves are generally the most important decisions leaders make, these moves must be made carefully and strategically; thus chess, not checkers.

We recommend a multidimensional team ranking process based upon three criteria: achievement of results, alignment with organizational values, and overall leadership qualities. We call this the Leadership Ranking.

Winning leaders know that the ideal team produces great results, is aligned with the organization's values, and has strong leadership, thus creating a bright future for the organization.

With this process completed and with the Leadership and the Position Rankings in alignment, winning leaders separate themselves from the rest more than with any other single tactic of which we are aware.

Where do most leaders spend the bulk of their time? Yes, with the C-Players. This leaves the A-Players feeling undervalued and likely leaves them underdeveloped.

Winning leaders spend more personalized time with A-Players than any other group, followed by C-Players, then B-Players.

Winning leaders share a philosophy of replacement leadership. They are always developing their replacement. They view it as their duty to the organization, but also as a way to strengthen and challenge the team in new directions.

Winning leaders manage people unequally. They believe that leadership is not "one size fits all" and that it is more complex because what works to lead each team member may be different.

Winning leaders take the time to find out what works for each individual while finding their hot buttons and pushing them.

Other leaders may make the mistake of developing a style and expecting everyone to adapt to it. Winning leaders adapt to the circumstance and the players who are working to maximize the performance of each team member. People are unique, and to lead them you must manage them unequally.

IMPORTANCE GAP

PART **2**

IMPORTANCE GAPS

6

IDENTIFYING
IMPORTANCE GAPS

Importance Gaps are the gaps between knowing an action and knowing its importance.

This is an area where the clarity of leaders is tested. With all that is asked of team members and leaders and all of the conflicting priorities and messages, things can fall through the cracks. Those things, of course, are Performance Gaps. Leaders need to make sure that the things that do inevitably fall through the cracks are never the big things.

"Importance Gaps are owned by the leader and are most often caused by a leader's lack of clarity."

Remember that Importance Gaps are created when someone knows what needs to be done and knows how to do it, but they don't take action because they don't feel consciously or subconsciously that it is important enough.

Importance Gaps are owned by the leader and are most often caused by a leader's lack of clarity.

This is another area where winning leaders separate themselves from the rest. Their teams know what is important!

Importance Gaps are often packaged as excuses like these:

- "We just didn't get to it. We ran out of time."

- "You gave me so much other stuff to do."

- "There are only twenty-four hours in a day! I will do it tomorrow."

- "I thought it was optional!"

- "I covered it at the meeting, but for some reason my team did not execute."

To illustrate Importance Gaps, let's come back to the example from Maddy's team. You may recall that her team of ten sales managers produced only $4.5 million in period one, missing the sales plan by $500,000. She identified and closed significant Knowledge Gaps in herself and her team. Her sales manager team is now aware of and was fully briefed on the three-step process that is to be executed by all sales reps to achieve the sales plan in period two.

We rejoin the team's progress as period two comes to a close. Maddy is very disappointed to find that against the same sales plan of $5 million, her team has once again missed it and produced only $4.8 million. So, there was progress from the $4.5 million in period one, but Maddy's team is still not meeting expectations.

With the Knowledge Gaps around the three-step process closed, Maddy is surprised that her team did not achieve the sales plan for period two. A surprised leader is never a good thing. She believes that they are a good team and have the ability to achieve and exceed the sales plan. Maddy assumed that by closing the Knowledge Gaps, all was well.

Let's take a look at the period one and two sales results in Figure 10.

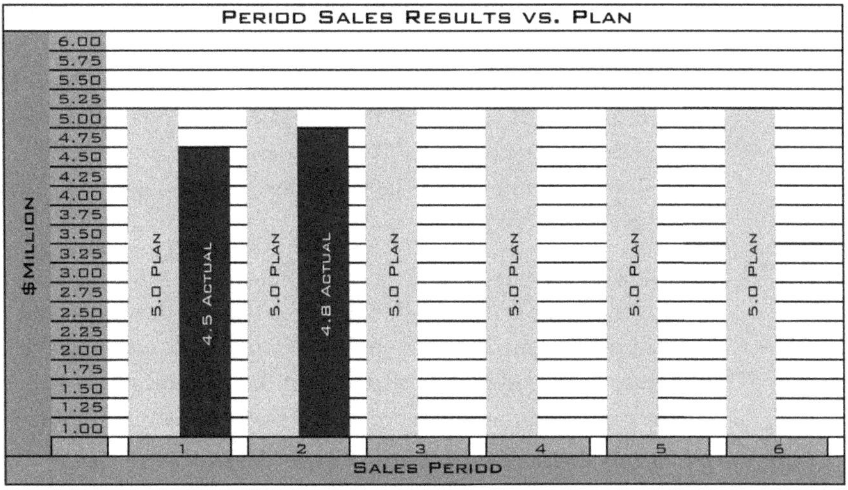

FIGURE 10 - PERIODS ONE AND TWO SALES

To identify the current Performance Gaps in herself and her team, she brings the sales managers together in a meeting to autopsy the period two performance results.

She asks the team the following questions:

- What commitments did the team make for period two?

- Which sales managers and reps made the sales plan for period two?

- What tactics did they use to make the sales plan?

- Which sales managers and reps missed the plan for period two?

- What gaps did they have in the three-step process?

In her autopsy and discussion of period two, she finds the following Importance Gaps and other facts:

- Once again, the same six of the ten sales managers made their sales plan, and therefore the same four sales managers did not.

- All of the six making their sales plan had met with their sales rep teams to role-play the three-step process, and chart on the Habit Ladder each rep's progress. The four who missed the sales plan had either emailed the process to their sales reps or covered it on a conference call or both. The Habit Ladder was not used to measure the sales rep's progress. This has created significant Importance

Gaps with their sales rep teams. They do not know it is a nonnegotiable execution point with each customer, as it was not role-played or demonstrated firsthand. The outcome created by these Importance Gaps is that the four sales managers missed their sales plan by a combined $400,000 in period two and had already missed period one by $700,000. Importance Gaps are very expensive!

- In reviewing the tactics of the six sales managers making the plan, it is clear that they executed the three-step process flawlessly, and it worked as evidenced by the results. They each had numerous customer success stories to share about the process and how they closed gaps with their sales rep teams that resulted in substantial sales. Therefore, there are no gaps with the three-step process. Importance Gaps closed!

- In reviewing the tactics of the four who missed sales plan, it was evident that the three-step process was not fully executed. This would have been evident at any point during the period with appropriate follow up on current behavior or results. It appears that a majority of the forty sales reps who work for the four sales managers do not understand the critical importance of executing the three-step process. Importance Gaps!

So, are the gaps with Maddy, the four sales managers, or both? How can she get the team to fully execute the three-step process so they will make the sales plan in period three?

The Knowledge Gaps appear to have been closed at the sales manager level, but not necessarily at the sales rep level. Based on this evidence, Maddy concludes that she is dealing with a lingering Knowledge Gaps at the sales rep level and Importance Gaps at the sales manager level. All of the sales managers had knowledge of the three-step process, but some of them failed to spread the importance and nonnegotiable status of the process to their team of sales reps.

These are classic examples of Importance Gaps, and they illustrate why closing the Knowledge Gaps alone may not lead to action. The knowledge and importance of the three-step process must be spread to the sales rep team, achieving Habit Level. The sales rep level can't have gaps on the three-step process! The customer has responded to the three-step process where executed. We know that is true because the six sales managers who drove the execution of the three-step process down through their sales reps exceeded the sales plan. The three-step selling process may be the best tactic ever developed within XYZ, but that does not matter unless it is fully understood, practiced, and executed.

Additional Importance Gaps were identified with Maddy herself. She did not see the evidence of gaps in both sales results and team behavior during period two. Instead, she assumed all was well since the three-step process had been communicated and the Knowledge Gaps were closed with the sales managers. She did not pay close attention to sales trends by each sales manager and had not observed the behavior of sales reps that were missing the sales plan. The Importance Gaps were obvious! The behaviors alone exposed the Performance Gaps, which in this case were glaring Importance Gaps. Now, Maddy must take swift action to close these Importance Gaps and create a positive outcome in period three! Time is running out.

The power of understanding and executing Gapology is that you can close specific gaps that can't be reopened. For example, if you were trained in a process and you confirm your understanding and model the behavior, it will be difficult for you to then claim a lack of knowledge of the process.

Do you see any potential lingering Knowledge Gaps?

Yes, the sales reps who work for the four sales managers appear to have Knowledge Gaps. They do not have a full understanding of the three-step process and are unlikely to know the success that other reps are having as a result of executing the process. It is doubtful they have climbed the Habit Ladder very far.

Are the four sales managers being fair to their sales reps? Are they inadvertently lowering their performance, compensation, and career potential? It would appear so. Put yourself in the reps' shoes. If you were a potentially top-performing sales rep, would you want to work for the four sales managers who did not fully share the benefits of the three-step process and role-play the steps with you until you were proficient at it? Compare these managers' behaviors with the others who insisted their reps achieve Habit Level execution of the three-step process. Gapology will shed light on gaps that you may not have been looking for.

Is it possible that the four sales managers' inability to execute the three-step process is an indicator of other performance issues? Recurring Knowledge and Importance Gaps highlight possible performance issues. These performance issues may not have been obvious before your understanding of Gapology.

You may conclude in this case that the four sales managers who missed plan in periods one and two should not be on Maddy's team. If you have concluded this, you may be right, but it is incumbent upon Maddy to close her own personal Performance Gaps first. By closing her own Knowledge and Importance Gaps, she will expose the true performance and the Performance Gaps of the four sales managers.

Winning Leader Behaviors to Identify Importance Gaps

- *Review results versus expectations.*
- *Observe behavior versus expectations.*
- *Ask about key expectations.*
- *Listen for understanding and commitment to the expectations.*
- *Avoid blame. Their answers may reflect your leadership.*
- *Restate expectations and ask for commitment.*

GAPOLOGY LESSONS
IDENTIFYING IMPORTANCE GAPS

Importance Gaps are the gaps between knowing an action and knowing its importance.

This is an area where the clarity of leaders is tested. With all that is asked of team members and leaders and all of the conflicting priorities and messages, things can fall through the cracks. Those things, of course, are Performance Gaps. Leaders need to make sure that the things that do inevitably fall through the cracks are never the big things.

Importance Gaps are often packaged as excuses like these:

- "We just didn't get to it. We ran out of time."
- "You gave me so much other stuff to do."
- "There are only twenty-four hours in a day! I will do it tomorrow."
- "I thought it was optional!"
- "I covered it at the meeting, but for some reason my team did not execute."

Winning Leader Behaviors to Identify Importance Gaps

- *Review results versus expectations.*
- *Observe behavior versus expectations.*
- *Ask about key expectations.*
- *Listen for understanding and commitment to the expectations.*
- *Avoid blame. Their answers may reflect your leadership.*
- *Restate expectations and ask for commitment.*

7

CLOSING IMPORTANCE GAPS

Closing Importance Gaps is a leader's role.

Winning leaders are strong and clear about what matters. They make sure there is no room for doubt. In the absence of a leader's clarity about what is important, chaos fills the gap, and that chaos leads to gaps in productivity and performance.

"Winning leaders make mistakes, but what separates them is that they learn from the mistakes and then intentionally adjust their behaviors to prevent them from recurring."

So, here are the actions Maddy took to close the Importance Gaps in an effort to make the sales plan in period three:

- She brought the four sales managers who missed sales plan in period two to her office to discuss period three and the three-step process execution. She did this as a group process.

- She expressed disappointment but accepted blame for her lack of follow up on their execution of the three steps.

- She reviewed the success of the three-step process where executed by the other six sales managers, and she cited two of the success stories.

- She asked for their commitment in executing the three-step process, achieving Habit Level execution, and achieving the sales plan in period three.

- She asked what consequences should be exercised if the process is not fully executed in period three.

- She agreed to those consequences and expressed her commitment to the plan.

- She attended a meeting with each sales manager and their sales reps to review and role-play the three-step process. She participated in the role-play herself.

- She brought a poster size Habit Ladder and had each rep role-play until they achieved Habit Level, then signed their name on the top step of the ladder! No one could leave until Habit Level was achieved and signed.

- She developed and executed a weekly follow-up strategy for measuring the execution of the three-step process by each sales manager and sales rep.

- She developed a Teachable Point of View about the three-step process for delivery when she meets with sales managers, sales reps, and customers.

- She also added a meeting with all new sales reps once per month to ensure their understanding and commitment to the three-step process, including Habit Level execution.

Do you think Maddy has finally made the execution of the three-step process important?

Do you think she got the attention of the four sales managers and their sales reps?

We think so. Importance Gaps closed. Hopefully, all Knowledge Gaps are closed, too. She has learned painful and costly lessons about Performance Gaps and is in a much stronger position to achieve the sales plan in period three than in periods one and two, now that her team is $700,000 in the hole.

Winning leaders make mistakes, but what separates them from others is that they learn from the mistakes and then intentionally adjust their behaviors to prevent them from recurring. We don't have hard proof, but based on our conversations with them, we believe that winning leaders make more mistakes than others because they take more risks. Playing it safe rarely leads to winning.

Because the Knowledge and Importance Gaps are closed, the four sales managers can't play the "importance card" again. They can't say, "We didn't know we had to execute the three-step process. We thought it was optional." There is no turning back when you get good at closing gaps. The power of moving left to right should be evident to you in this example.

Winning leaders close Knowledge Gaps first. Closing Importance Gaps is built upon that foundation, leaving action as the most likely outcome. And that means that great performance and great results are just around the corner.

Closed Knowledge Gaps and Importance Gaps set up teams to win! They know what to do, how to do it, when to do it, and why it matters. That is the world winning leaders create.

Winning Leader Behaviors to Close Importance Gaps

> *Review results versus expectations.*
>
> *Observe team behavior versus expectations.*
>
> *Declare the Importance Gap.*
>
> *Accept blame and reset expectations.*
>
> *Ask for commitment and agree to the consequences for inaction.*
>
> *Follow up and verify commitments.*

GAPOLOGY LESSONS
CLOSING IMPORTANCE GAPS

Closing Importance Gaps is a leader's role.

Winning leaders are strong and clear about what matters. They make sure there is no room for doubt. In the absence of a leader's clarity about what is important, chaos fills the gap, and that chaos leads to gaps in productivity and performance.

Winning Leader Behaviors to Close Importance Gaps

- *Review results versus expectations.*
- *Observe team behavior versus expectations.*
- *Declare the Importance Gap.*
- *Accept blame and reset expectations.*
- *Ask for commitment and agree to the consequences for inaction.*
- *Follow up and verify commitments.*

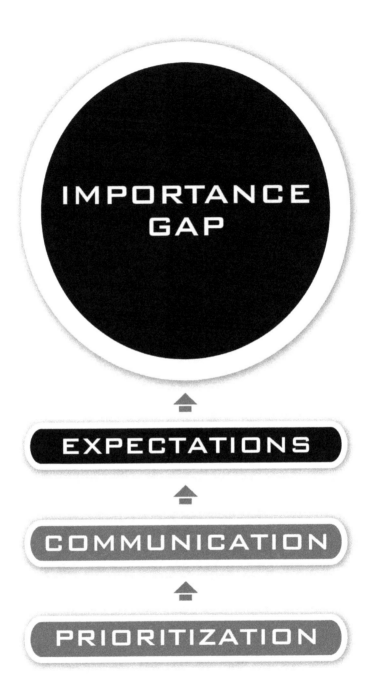

8

EXPECTATIONS
ROOT SOLUTION

Let's start by dispelling the myth that expectations are simply goals. They aren't. Many leaders make the mistake of setting goals, but not expectations.

> "Expectations are the things that the leader 'expects' to be delivered and are nonnegotiable."

Winning leaders know to do both. They are different. Goals are things to strive for. They are nice to have. They are targets and may be long range. Expectations are the things that the leader "expects" to be delivered and are nonnegotiable. They are "must-haves," and winning leaders create accountability around expectations.

When you establish a sales budget or plan, you expect it to be achieved. It is not something you wish for. You likely commit to your superiors that financial expectation. From there, you build an expense budget that delivers an expected profit. These are nonnegotiable. Everyone on the team must be all in on meeting his or her allotted portion of the plan.

A goal is much different. You may create a goal of beating the sales budget by 10 percent, setting 110 percent of the sales budget as the goal. This would be nice to have, but is not the same as the nonnegotiable expectation. Everyone on the team should work to achieve the goal, but it is much different than the expectation.

Winning leaders require expectations to have both a behavioral and a result component.

As shown in the Expectations Model, Figure 11, the expected result must be determined by verifying which behaviors will produce it and vice versa. The expected behaviors must produce the expected result. They must work together. They are symbiotic and cannot stand-alone. Often, leaders will set one or the other, but not both. They will provide the expected result but not the expected behavior that will actually produce that result. Or they will just focus on the behaviors but remain unclear about what expected result they want to see.

Let's take Maddy's team as an example. Maddy expects the three-step selling process to be executed by all sales reps with all customers. That would be the behavioral component. It can be observed and its steps measured. It is not optional, and the execution of it is expected with every customer.

She also has evidence that when executed at Habit Level with every customer the sales plan is achieved. Therefore, achieving the sales plan is an expectation and represents the result component of the three-step process expectation.

Winning leaders are confident that when the behavioral component of an expectation is met, the result component will follow. They test it and have examples of where the behavior was executed and the result followed.

The power in setting clear expectations is achieved by winning leaders through the transfer of ownership. Once the team knows their expectations and has committed to them, the leader has successfully transferred ownership of those expectations.

It is like the quarterback handing off the ball to the running back. Once the ball is secure in the running back's hands, the quarterback has transferred ownership to the running back. The quarterback may still need to throw a block or two, but the transfer is complete. The quarterback needed to have made a good play call, and the quarterback still owns the game score, but the ball is in the hands of the running back. It is then up to the running back to perform.

Winning leaders have learned to play the role of a great quarterback.

FIGURE 11 - EXPECTATIONS MODEL

GAPS WITH YOUR BOSS

We have found that many leaders miss the Importance Gaps that exist with their own boss. They are not clear on what their boss expects. Winning leaders own this, even if the boss doesn't. Some bosses just aren't good at sharing clear expectations, so they create gaps with the leaders who report to them. Winning leaders don't let this stand in their way. They find out what the bosses expectations are, period! No gaps!

Do you want to be the boss someday? Allowing the boss's limitations to stand in your way does not set you up for promotion. The quickest way to get promoted is to get the boss promoted! So it is critical that you always know your boss's expectations, his or her vision of great. This allows you to exceed expectations and create a vision of great that may that may lead the boss to an even higher set of expectations. This one tactic will help the boss get promoted faster than any other.

Sometimes the boss does not have high expectations. Creating the vision of great for your boss and the rest of the team puts you in a strong position! Be the one that fills the void and leads everyone forward. This may lead to your promotion.

ONE HUNDRED PERCENT EXECUTION

One hundred percent execution refers to tasks and processes that you and your team nail 100 percent of the time. It is that critical set of nonnegotiable expectations called out and made clear by leadership. Most leaders get a blank look when asked about things they do 100 percent of the time. But we have found that winning leaders view 100 percent execution as not only possible, but also a common expectation.

An example of 100 percent execution comes from the airline industry. For those of you who fly regularly, you are likely very happy that airlines operate at Six Sigma (similar to 100 percent execution) in most operational functions. Six Sigma is a level of execution equal to 3.4 exceptions per one million attempts. That is why you could fly every day of your entire lifetime on US commercial airlines and never experience a plane crash.

It is also reassuring to know that most restaurants do a lot of things relating to food safety 100 percent of the time, so it is an execution reality. It may require built in redundancies and triple check mechanisms, but you can do it. So when you think of setting expectations and when you are challenging your team, consider 100 percent execution a reality. Challenge the team on the execution points that they commit to delivering and measuring 100 percent of the time.

Most leaders set goals, but not expectations. Most expectations can actually be executed 100 percent of the time, if that becomes the leader's expectation and that expectation is passed on to the team.

Next is an exercise for you to use and a restaurant example that demonstrates the 100 percent execution strategy:

100 PERCENT EXECUTION EXERCISE

Business Case:	Every organization has key items that must be executed 100 percent of the time and have success examples that can be applied to the areas where there are Performance Gaps.
Items Needed:	Paper/flipchart/dry erase board with markers
Steps:	
1	List tasks where 100 percent execution is currently achieved.
2	Determine and list the reasons why 100 percent execution occurs for these tasks.
3	List tasks where 100 percent execution is not being achieved but is expected.
4	Determine and list actions leaders must take to achieve 100 percent execution to close these gaps.

THINGS WE DO 100 PERCENT OF THE TIME	WHY THEY MUST BE 100 PERCENT EXECUTED
Make bank deposit	Expectation of putting the money in the bank
Open the doors for business	Expectation to allow guests to enter
Wash the dishes	Expectation of clean plates for our guests
Take out the trash	Expectation of a clean environment
Wipe down the tables after the guests finish eating	Expectation that each guest has a clean experience
THINGS WE NEED TO DO 100 PERCENT OF THE TIME	**LEADER ACTIONS TO GET TO 100 PERCENT EXECUTION**
Servers recommend desserts every time	Train, set clear expectations measure results, create accountability and consequences
Servers recommend the "special" every time	Train, set clear expectations measure results, create accountability and consequences
Food at state-required temperatures	Measure temperature readings
Consistent food preparation	Train, set clear expectations measure results, create accountability and consequences
Complaints are handled quickly and thoroughly	Monitor complaints, coach team on proper handling, set clear expectations, measure results, create accountability and consequences

SETTING CLEAR EXPECTATIONS

I learned the power of setting clear expectations early in my career. I had been promoted to district manager of a sales team in Southern California. My boss, the VP of Sales, escorted me to a meeting to introduce me to my new team of sales reps and support staff. As we pulled into the parking lot of the hotel where the meeting was being held, he warned me of a "bad apple," John. He said, "John needs to be fired. His sales market area has great potential, but he has poor customer standards and terrible results, and he has not responded to my coaching at all. Get rid of him!"

That was a very strong statement, but after meeting John and talking to him about his business and what he was proud of, it was clear that my boss was likely right about John. Each of the sales managers gave a fifteen-minute overview of their sales, customer metrics, and focus for the remainder of the year. John's presentation lacked energy and clarity. As you might expect, John's sales were poor, and his customer service scores were the worst in the market. It looked like John would not make the team going forward.

I scheduled a meeting with John for later that week. We spent the whole day together. We talked about his poor results and what he thought was the root cause. I reviewed my expectations and the tactics that would deliver those expectations. We also met with our top clients in John's market and listened to their needs and expectations. John was engaged and knowledgeable. I was surprised. He took detailed notes and asked questions. I expressed that achieving result expectations is nonnegotiable. I was very clear about John's need to execute to our standards, exceed our customer's expectations, and through these things achieve result expectations.

At about seven o'clock in the evening, we sat down for a recap of the day. I asked him for his summary and asked what he needed from me. After recapping the expectations, he said, "You just gave me exactly what I needed today. I have worked here for ten years and have never had anyone so clearly lay out expectations or spend the day with me. Thank you." He had tears in his eyes.

We shook hands, and I left not sure what to think. John seemed to have something in him, an inner spark that did not match my boss's impression or John's poor results. I was unsure of what this meant, but that inner spark gave me a glimmer of hope. The bottom line was that John was clear on expectations. He was capable of executing, so the ball was now in his court.

I visited with John the following week and observed his customer interaction. Something had changed. John's service level and standards of execution had jumped considerably. I was surprised, but then again I wasn't. That inner spark was there, so had it been ignited? Was this just temporary?

John never returned to the days of low standards and poor service. He never looked back. Within one year John established himself as the top sales rep in the district. I sent all new hires and struggling reps to spend time with John to learn how an area should be operated and to see what great looked like. He had outstanding results and fabulous standards.

You couldn't wipe the smile off John's face. One day, backstage at the annual awards celebration, I asked John what he was doing differently that was creating such outstanding results.

He laughed and said, "You don't know?" I shook my head.

He said, "It is simple, just like you said it would be. I set very clear expectations for myself, every day, every week, and in every customer interaction. I train the new reps and those I mentor by starting and ending with a recap of expectations."

Now you couldn't wipe the smile off my face.

MADDY'S LEARNINGS

Winning leaders know that there is no substitute for setting clear expectations. Clear expectations go a long way in closing Importance Gaps. Leaders who do not set clear expectations put their team at a disadvantage. Setting clear expectations is the number one way to close Importance Gaps. Clear expectations are at the foundation of great performance.

GAPOLOGY LESSONS
EXPECTATIONS
ROOT SOLUTION

Let's start by dispelling the myth that expectations are simply goals. They aren't. Many leaders make the mistake of setting goals but not expectations. Winning leaders know to do both. Goals are things to strive for. They are nice to have. They are targets and may be long range. Expectations are the things that the leader "expects" to be delivered and are nonnegotiable. They are "must-haves," and winning leaders create accountability around expectations.

Winning leaders require expectations to have both a behavioral and a result component.

As shown in the Expectations Model, Figure 11, the expected result must be determined by verifying which behaviors will produce it and vice-versa. The expected behaviors must produce the expected result. They must work together. They are symbiotic and cannot stand-alone.

The power in setting clear expectations is achieved by winning leaders through the transfer of ownership. Once the team knows their expectations and has committed to them, the leader has successfully transferred ownership of those expectations.

We have found that many leaders miss the Importance Gaps that exist with their own boss. They are not clear on what their boss expects. Winning leaders own this, even if the boss doesn't. Some bosses just aren't good at sharing clear expectations, so they create gaps with their leaders. Winning leaders don't let this stand in their way. They find out what the boss's expectations are, period! No gaps!

Winning leaders know that there is no substitute for setting clear expectations Clear expectations go a long way in closing Importance Gaps. Leaders who do not set clear expectations put their team at a disadvantage.

9

COMMUNICATION
ROOT SOLUTION

As we have discussed, Importance Gaps are most often the result of the leader's lack of clear communication.

Just like recurring Knowledge Gaps imply a talent issue with a team member, recurring Importance Gaps imply a clarity and prioritization issue with the leader. There tends to be an overriding assumption by leaders who miss expectations that if something has been communicated, it is therefore understood and will be acted upon.

"Winning leaders assume nothing! They over communicate a clear message and ensure it is understood."

Winning leaders assume nothing! They over communicate a clear message and ensure it is understood. Winning leaders use communication as a tool to win and do not take it for granted. They carefully select the correct type of communication that will be most effective in delivering the desired result. Winning leaders leverage communication as a differentiator. It closes gaps. That is Gapology!

Clear, concise, and verified communication closes Importance Gaps. Winning leaders destroy the competition here. They select how they will communicate carefully. If a face-to-face meeting is required, they will not leave it to a phone call or an email. Winning leaders show great courage here and know that how a message is communicated is often as important as the message itself.

With today's variety of media, the type of communication media we choose matters. Leaders have many options, such as face-to-face discussions, phone calls, voice mails, emails, text messages, social media messaging, written notes or letters, conference calls, meetings, webinars, and many others.

Everything a leader does is under a microscope. Every action of a leader communicates importance to the team. Even the lack of action says something, so carefully select both your actions and how you communicate. Winning leaders use their actions and their communication to close Importance Gaps.

Winning leaders are very deliberate about communication. They are not random with communication because they know it impacts their team's behavior.

Each of these communication media has its limitations when it comes to creating action, but each can be effective when used appropriately and in combination with others. Which media you choose will have a big impact on whether you close the Importance Gaps or whether you become the gap.

Here are the effective aspects of different communication media and how winning leaders use each to close Importance Gaps and create action:

FACE-TO-FACE DISCUSSIONS

Face-to-face discussions are excellent for setting clear and concise expectations with one individual where quick action is required. These are rare today, due to the limited time most leaders have available, but they are by far the most powerful tools when you need to create significant action in an individual. Start by setting the stage, explaining what you will be speaking about. When applicable, make the business case and explain the bigger purpose of the action required. At the end of the conversation, ask questions to confirm the understanding of what must be done, how it must be done, why it is critical, and when it must be done.

Some face-to-face conversations need to be short and directive.

A simple model here is: Tell them what they need to know, tell them why it matters, and tell them what action is required from them and when it must be done. Turn the conversation back to the individual for a recap and any questions.

The downside of face-to-face discussions is that they take time. Depending on the size of your team and the geography they cover, these discussions may be impractical, but when there is no substitute for the clarity of a nodding head, face-to-face discussions get it done.

Body language is a great way to determine engagement, and for this reason it predicts future gaps and allows you to directly close Importance Gaps.

PERSONAL PHONE CALLS

Many of the same rules apply with personal phone calls as with face-to-face discussions, but phone calls come with greater limitations.

You can't see body language to confirm understanding or engagement, and they can't see yours. This makes it more difficult to communicate a strong message that will create the required action.

Here is a simple model to follow if you are attempting to create quick action with a team member: Start by setting expectations at the beginning of the call. Say, "Have you got a few minutes? Can you jot a few notes? I want to make sure you are clear on what needs to be done this week and the outcomes I am looking for." This will raise their engagement level, and they will certainly know the importance of the call. Make sure you verify understanding. Say, "Okay, walk me through what we have discussed. What must be done, how, when, and why?" Fill in any gaps. Listen for hesitancy or lack of commitment.

We suggest you fill gaps in your travel time to do phone calls, making sure you are safe and legal when doing so. Be aware of the limitations and the possibility of gaps with phone calls. Have follow-up mechanisms in place for any actions required. Assume nothing.

VOICE-MAILS

Be careful not to have any assumptions of understanding here. Voice-mails are hard to verify and will need to be combined with other media to be effective. They are not a reliable source of action creation.

We suggest you avoid them, other than to have the recipient call back. If that won't work, make your message narrow and clear, repeating the key points, and then follow up for understanding (for example, your follow up may be an email asking for confirmation that your message was received and understood).

EMAILS, TEXTS, AND SOCIAL MESSAGING

Emails, text messages, and social media messages are the fastest and most efficient method of communication, but they can be deceiving in terms of closing gaps. Unfortunately, they can create more gaps than they close, so be careful and clear.

The greatest strengths of emails and texts are speed and breadth. In five seconds, you can communicate the importance of an action to your entire team.

The greatest weakness of emails and texts is the false assumption that the recipient will understand your intent and that action will result. Do not fall into this gap!

Email and text messages will need to be combined with other media to be effective in creating action and closing gaps.

Examples include:

- Email or text, plus a follow-up call, email, or text from the recipient when the action is completed.

- Email or text, plus a follow-up call, email or text from the recipient recapping their understanding of the communication. This allows you to follow up on an exception basis only.

Leaders who rely too heavily on email or texts for communication of critical actions generally create significant Performance Gaps. Winning leaders do not assume their communication is effective. They verify that it has been effective.

Social media fits into this same category. Simple and tempting to use on our laptops and smartphones, this creates the same benefits and limitations as other electronic communication. Any social media site set up for the use of sharing information must have a catch net established for any important pieces that may slip through the cracks that need to be verified.

HANDWRITTEN NOTES AND LETTERS

Handwritten notes and letters are truly a lost art form. They tug at the heart-strings and may be cherished by the recipient. They are great for creating a personal touch and long-lasting engagement. Winning leaders use them for recognition, thanks, and creating shared vision around an initiative. They have a long table life!

I walked into an office recently, and there was my hand written note from five years ago pinned to the corner of a corkboard. How many times do you think the recipient read that note over the five years? Do you think the message had an impact?

Handwritten notes and letters are obviously limited in their effectiveness of communicating action and confirming understanding of the action to be taken. Generally, this is not their mission.

Use these to create an emotional connection with peers and team members, with an important initiative, and to create recognition around a critical result. Word will spread.

CONFERENCE CALLS

Conference calls and even video conferencing calls are among the most overrated of communication media. They are often necessary for work teams that are spread over significant geography, but they are extremely limiting and cause leaders to falsely assume understanding and action.

A best method we found to make conference calls more effective is the use of random recaps. A winning leader we know randomly calls on someone to recap which actions have been agreed to on the call. This can be done a few times during the call or just at the end, depending on the amount of material covered. It really keeps the team members on their toes and makes their notes very important. You can announce this protocol at the start of the call or make it part of your leadership rhythm routine for your direct reports. It is very effective.

You should also email a recap of actions agreed to at the end of the call and request a confirming email that the importance is understood and action will be taken.

MEETINGS

Meetings are also overrated in their effectiveness of closing gaps or creating action. Skilled leaders, however, can be effective using this method. Great meetings are only great meetings if they result in the desired action being taken.

Winning leaders only conduct meetings with a purpose and an objective, designed to create action in the team. They do not meet to just to meet.

Here are tactics that winning leaders use to turn meetings into action:

AGENDA

The most effective meetings have an agenda sent out in advance, laying out the purpose and objective of the meeting, plus any pre-work required. Pre-work is a great idea, if you are not already using it. It increases engagement and focus around the meeting. Executing this tactic begins closing the Importance Gap before the meeting has even started.

OBJECTIVE

State and then write the meeting objective on a white board or flip chart. Review the objective at the beginning of the meeting and throughout the meeting to seek feedback from the attendees on whether the objective is being met. Put the objective in the agenda as well.

RANDOM RECAPS

Similar to the conference call leader behavior, randomly call upon attendees to recap the key points and actions at intervals during the meeting. This keeps the team engaged and makes note taking advisable. The first time you do this, pick someone who will do a good job. Compliment them on their engagement level, and you will have set the bar for the team.

If an attendee does not have a complete recap, ask the group to fill in the blanks to ensure the message is clear. You will quickly know the engagement level of individual attendees. In any case, you will have heightened the ongoing engagement of the team. This is a winning leader tactic that is extremely effective.

CALLS TO ACTION

This is a great tactic we have witnessed firsthand. Bring the team close together at the end of the meeting, restate the objective, and declare your expectations. This can be very powerful and will close any potential Importance Gaps.

Follow this with attendees speaking to their commitment. Let volunteers go first, then call on those who did not speak. As they state their commitment, thank them and then ask them when they will achieve their commitment. This elevates the importance of the meeting and moves the team to action.

It is your role, as a leader, to follow up on the commitments made. An option is to write them down and send each attendee a follow-up letter or email listing their commitments and thanking them in advance for achieving them.

If every meeting is conducted in this manner, the team will come to the meeting knowing that the expectation of each meeting is action. They will know that when they leave, the meeting does not end. Action becomes the ongoing purpose. This is huge and can be a game changer! The team should be encouraged to model the same behavior in meetings with their teams. (See the "W" meeting structure later in this chapter.)

POST-MEETING ASSIGNMENTS

Post-meeting assignments are very effective at keeping the meeting alive and also turning it into action. Post-meeting assignments will make the meeting more important and set an expectation of action. Tie the assignments to results or measurable outcomes, post these outcomes, and create champions around them. This raises the stakes of the game and makes meetings more important because they become tied directly to action and results.

Using communication to close Importance Gaps is truly an art. Winning leaders connect their teams to the importance of their actions, and because of this, they perform at much higher levels.

There is no single type of communication that equals success, but the blending of the tactics reviewed in this chapter has been tested and proven to be effective. Winning leaders win with communication.

NO LEADER WITHOUT FOLLOWERS

By definition, if you are a leader, you must have followers.

Significant Performance Gaps in your team imply a lack of leadership and as a result create a lack of followership.

Performance Gaps exist because of the lack of clear leadership. Winning leaders create winning followers and other leaders.

We found certain "guideposts" winning leaders use to create a culture of followership:

MISSION STATEMENT

The mission statement of an organization is not for advertising to the customers, although many put it out on display. It is for the followers. Written properly, it becomes a road map or identity for what you want to achieve. It describes the big-picture outcome.

It is not a catch phrase or an ad slogan. It is true north on the compass and it is therefore directional. If you can write one that is inspirational, you can create followers. An organization's leadership must live up to its mission statement, or it becomes just words for others to follow.

Winning organizations have a strong mission, understood by all, and create an energy and focus. For the winning leaders and their organizations, mission statements are about clarity of direction. They help close Importance Gaps and allow team members to make the right decisions, aligned with the mission.

Mission statements put everyone in the organization on the same page and not on their own agenda. This is a key to winning performance

ORGANIZATIONAL VALUES

Values are key to any organization's sustained success. Organizational values describe what the organization believes in and who they are at heart. Like the mission statement, these values should be inspirational, but they may also be aspirational.

We suggest that they be added to the annual review process and measured. Each team member's behavior should be measured as either meeting or not meeting the values, and the term "hero" should be reserved for those who go above and beyond by teaching the values to others. If a team member does not meet the values, his or her career may be in jeopardy.

Organizational values should be used not only to measure behavior but also to help the decision-making process. Aligning your decisions with your values is a great and teachable practice.

Organizational values can also become a source of great pride for the team members. People like to work for a company that stands for something and is not just concerned about profit. This is enhanced when the top leaders truly live and breathe the values.

From a Gapology standpoint, values help close Importance Gaps by keeping it clear what the organization values and finds important.

LEADERSHIP COMPETENCIES

Leadership Competencies are key to developing strong teams with sustained results. They are the skills that the leadership team needs to possess to be successful.

Leadership competencies are important to use in hiring new team members and leaders. Interview guides should be created to align the questions with both the organizational values and the leadership competencies.

Let's say that your organization is going through a time of great change. The industry is consolidating, and you may be merging with another organization. The leadership competency of Embracing Change is a required key skill for all leaders to succeed. You should interview to it, hire to it, and teach and train it to the leaders.

We suggest that you define the top leadership competencies for your organization, and work hard to teach and evaluate your team within them.

Interview guides should include key questions around each competency so key leadership candidates are being matched to these competencies.

These can also be a key part of your teaching organization and the topic of Teachable Points of View of leadership.

WINNING LEADER COMPETENCIES

We found that the following eight competencies best capture those possessed by winning leaders and represent a strong force in closing Performance Gaps:

EMBRACING CHANGE

This leader will close Knowledge and Importance Gaps during times of change by leading the team through the uncertainty. She will model strong behavior.

MANAGERIAL COURAGE

This leader will ensure that the team takes the appropriate actions and will remove underperformers from the team. He will deliver the tough message when needed. This competency closes Action Gaps.

COMMUNICATOR

This leader will deliver a strong message that others can take as their own. She will keep the team on track and focused on the right stuff. This competency is crucial to the success of a leader because it is required to close all gaps. Someone without this competency will never become a winning leader.

RESULTS-DRIVEN

This leader will take an assignment and deliver the desired outcome. He will close Action Gaps with his team and himself.

MOTIVATOR

This leader will lead her team to sustained results. She will keep Importance Gaps closed through her strong point of view. She will also lead the team to victory by closing Action Gaps.

ACTIVE LISTENER

This leader listens before speaking and leads with questions, not answers. He will be in touch with his team and keep Knowledge and Importance Gaps closed.

RESPONSIBLE

This leader does not pass the buck. She will own the outcome and take responsibility when things don't go as expected. She will have a strong sense of ownership for results and will close Action Gaps.

COMPETITIVE

This leader loves to win and sees that as the mission. He will publish results, and his team members will always know where they stand. He can be counted on to close Importance and Action Gaps with his team.

SIMPLICITY

In the Introduction, we shared the organizational structure of the sales team at XYZ. You will note that it is very simple. There are only three layers between the president of the company, Tom Case, and the front-line sales reps that interface directly with the customer.

This example of simplicity is a competitive advantage for XYZ. Simplicity in structure improves communication. Performance is enhanced in a simple structure. Action becomes automatic because the action is up to you. It can't be passed off as someone else's job. Communication also flows from the top to the bottom and the bottom to the top without interpretation or interruption. Extra layers can add support and expertise, but they can also create confusion, mixed messages, and productivity issues.

Have you ever played the game where a phrase is told to one person, who tells the next, and so on? By the time it circles back to the person who started the phrase, it is much different.

This is what happens in organizations with excessive layers, but in business it's not a game. Layers can be a root cause of poor performance, which is somewhat counter-logical. Each individual on each level has a personal filter that screens out communicated information that they consciously or unconsciously deem as unimportant or irrelevant to their role. This problem compounds as more layers are added and you actually end up spending more on salaries and overhead to get less done and deliver inadequate or week communication and ultimately poorer results.

Winning leaders make the layers of structure irrelevant. They develop communication methods that keep it simple and create clarity around expectations and importance.

During our interviews with winning leaders and their teams, we found the following generalities:

KNOWLEDGE GAPS DID NOT EXIST

The team knows what to do and how to do it. These teams seem to have fewer turnovers, so they are familiar with each other. The team was chosen wisely, and everyone knew his or her role. They were committed to winning and were clear on that definition. Everyone on the team knew about their success, and they each knew that they owned a piece of that success.

IMPORTANCE GAPS WERE MINIMAL

The leader kept the focus narrow and published the critical results daily, weekly, and for the period. Accountability was divided up between the team, and they supported each other in being successful. Everyone knew what was expected. They described both the behavioral expectations and the result expectations. Underperformers were coached to improve and removed from the team quickly if they did not meet expectations. There was very little competition within the team. Instead, they competed as a team against their own expectations and took great pride in their performance.

ACTION GAPS WERE NOT NOTICEABLE

The team owned its own actions. The leader was organized and had a plan to get the required things done. On the rare occasions when the team got behind, a plan was developed and executed to catch up immediately. This action orientation was essential in creating winning results.

Winning leaders make simplicity a priority and fundamental to the way they conduct their business.

On the next page, you will find an exercise to complete that is designed to illustrate Simplicity. By taking a thorough look at your organization and its communication structure, you may discover new ways to minimize the risk of creating Importance Gaps. Use XYZ's organization as an example:

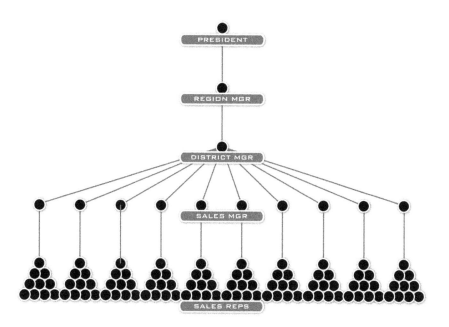

SIMPLICITY EXERCISE	
Business Case:	Winning leaders use simplicity to create great communication that leads to great performance.
Items Needed:	Paper/flipchart/dry erase board with markers Organizational chart
Steps:	
1	On the flipchart draw out your organizational hierarchy. List all levels from the top-ranked leader all the way to the customer in a straight downward path.
2	Connect all levels with a line indicating the flow of communication.
3	Observe any lines that lead in any direction other than straight down.
4	These horizontal lines represent a potential interruption of the communication flow from the leader of the organization to the customer.
5	Determine how communication flows through these positions in order to ensure clear communication is executed. Determine the value of these positions as compared to the potential risk to the communication flow.
6	Streamline the communication flow by eliminating these interruption points or adjusting how the information is being communicated to the layers below.

INTENSITY W

We got this great tactic from The Rolling Stones! Thanks, Mick!

The Gapology team had seats that were side stage at The Rolling Stones concert. The seats were good enough to be near the Plexiglas box that Charlie Watts, the Stones' drummer, sat in. Written on the inside of the Plexiglas box with a grease pencil was the set list or the songs in playing order for the show. They were backward to us, but we could make out the first one and the last one very clearly.

We were curious. What was the relevance of the order? So, what do you think the first and last songs were?

We will tie this back to The Rolling Stones in a moment.

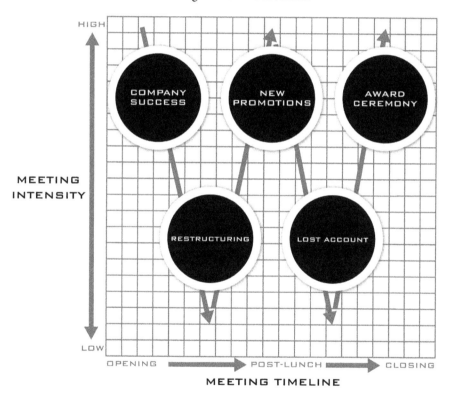

FIGURE 12 - INTENSITY W - MEETING STRUCTURE

The Intensity W - Meeting Structure, Figure 12, works for full or half-day meetings and structured conference calls or webinars. It works for any event where engagement of the audience matters. The concept is simple. View the W as an intensity meter vertically and a timeline horizontally.

There are three vertical high-intensity points: the beginning, the middle, and the end. There are two low points: one between the beginning and middle and the other between the middle and the end.

People remember two parts of a meeting more than any others: the opening and the closing. It is the same for concerts. Well-timed intensity increases excitement, engagement, and comprehension.

The Rolling Stones opened with *Jumping Jack Flash* and closed with "Brown Sugar" because they are the highest-intensity, crowd-pleasing rock songs. On an intensity meter, that would look like a V. What the Stones did was create an additional spike of intensity in the middle, thus a W. They created the middle spike of intensity by moving to the middle of the arena onto a destination stage, where they wrapped up a set featuring *It's Only Rock and Roll.* Slower songs like *Angie* and *Wild Horses* created the low points in the concert, and they served to make the spikes in intensity seem even higher by creating a contrast.

You can do the same thing with your meetings. There are a few ways to accomplish this. One way would be to rank your meeting agenda items in intensity and simply put the top three into the opening, middle, and closing slots.

Another way is to create intensity with your meeting design. For example, you could open with a clever and interactive introductory game, move to recognition and performance awards right after lunch, then close with a strong speaker who pulls it all together and creates a call to action.

Another variation we have found successful for all-day meetings is a V first half, and then another V in the second half. The difference here is that you bring the intensity up four times versus just three. The additional intense agenda item is added just before lunch. This can cause some significant buzz and positive conversation during the lunch hour and increase engagement as they come back to another intense topic.

We've discovered the benefits of using this method for training workshops, face-to-face meetings, performance reviews, sales presentations, and any type of important communication where high levels of engagement are essential and action is required. This really works, and it closes Importance Gaps!

Winning leaders use well-timed intensity to move teams to action.

The exercise shown on the following pages illustrates Maddy's "W" Meeting Structure strategy. You can use this process to plan out the flow of your meetings. By following the "W" thought process, you will begin to apply intensity at crucial moments and create impact like never before.

INTENSITY W EXERCISE	
Business Case:	Creating a business rhythm by structuring your meetings/conference calls to maximize their impact.
Items Needed:	Meeting/conference call agenda Horizontal timeline
Steps:	
1	Begin by listing all topics to be covered during a meeting, conference call, etc. and the approximate amount of time needed to cover each topic.
2	Rank each of the topics in order of emotional intensity.
3	While considering the amount of time needed, position the three topics with the highest emotional intensity at the top of the "W" lines.
4	Position the two topics with the lowest emotional intensity at the two bottom points of the "W."
5	Continue to position the remaining topics throughout the "W" timeline, taking into consideration the positioning of any break and lunch times if being used to structure a meeting.
6	If used in a meeting situation, remember the post-lunch doldrums. Positioning a "pick-me-up" at multiple intervals in the afternoon helps to keep the group lively.

FILL YOURS OUT HERE:

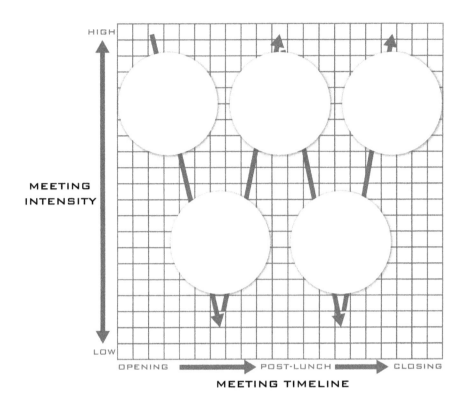

THE STANDING OVATION

Recently, I attended a meeting with an underperforming sales manager and their sales rep team. They ranked in the bottom 10 percent of the company in performance, therefore the C-Group we have talked so much about. The C-Group is often filled with a majority of C-Players, which we discussed in the chapter on Talent. These C-Players often have potential but are being held back by a C-Leader, so I was curious.

The purpose of their meeting was to role-play selling behaviors specifically modeling the three-step process. They were to have best method presentations by the top performers on the team to help the entire team move to Habit Level.

As I observed their behavior and listened to their conversations, it was clear to me that their bottom 10 percent ranking was justified. They were sarcastic, cynical, and were at best unenthusiastic. They didn't seem to be motivated by serving the customer or helping each other succeed. C-Players surround themselves with C-Players. Losing finds comfort there. This team appeared to be just collecting paychecks and going through the motions. How could they be part of my team?

As I spent time talking to team members individually during lunch and on breaks, I found that they were different than my initial assessment. They were intelligent, caring, and had some understanding of our vision. They were knowledgeable about the company and were clear about the district expectations.

I was perplexed that their behavior and their results were so different from what they articulated individually. I quickly ruled out Knowledge Gaps as the big issue and realized that I was dealing with Importance Gaps.

Clearly, the leader was not creating an adequate sense of urgency around results. This team simply didn't view the company or district expectations as important. They saw these expectations as stretch goals. They were satisfied with their performance. Since I was there, I decided to take action to move the team forward.

At the end of the meeting I brought the team together, and we stood in a circle and just talked. I asked if they knew how their collective performance ranked within the district. They weren't clear. Each of them had a different answer. I informed them of their bottom 10 percent performance and expressed my disappointment. They agreed that their performance was unacceptable. This was a good sign. True disappointment was expressed, and that's a start. I'm sure they thought a reprimand was coming from me, but it was not. I decided to try something different, much different.

As we stood there in the circle, I asked each of them to tell the group of a time when they had performed at a high level and had received a standing ovation. I gave them time to think about their past successes.

Aaron went first. He had been the starting tight end of his high school football team during his senior year. Although the team did not a have a very good year, he caught the winning touchdown pass to beat their crosstown rivals. He said the crowd cheered for what felt like minutes. He said that this was his only experience with being on the receiving end of a standing ovation. You could see that moment beam in his face as he relived the catch. We repeated the cheering by giving Aaron another standing ovation. It was an enthusiastic burst of energy from the whole group. You could see the impact in Aaron's face. It felt good.

Trisha went next. She was the valedictorian at her high school and had delivered a speech on leadership and how each graduate could make a difference in the world. When she completed the speech, the crowd and students rose to their feet and applauded and cheered. She said it was the highlight of her life, and tears poured down her cheeks as she spoke. We gave Trisha another standing ovation, and the tears continued.

Jose went next. He reluctantly admitted that he had never received a standing ovation. I asked the team if Jose had ever done anything at work deserving of a standing ovation. Everyone jumped in with different stories about how Jose had helped him or her take care of a customer. We proudly gave Jose a rousing standing ovation. Jose beamed. He said he felt like a hero!

We continued this process until everyone on the team had received a personal standing ovation. Then we talked about things in their environment that were worthy of a standing ovation. They came up with five different examples of behavior that fit their criteria. We talked about how they could give standing ovations in the workplace and quickly developed a plan to change the motivation of their team, making performance really important.

I asked each of them for their commitment to achieving expectations. We went back around the circle until we had a sincere, "I'm in!" from everyone. It felt good, but only their behavior change would change the results.

Things changed for that team that day. They saw things differently and began to appreciate each other's performance. They moved from the bottom of the pack to the middle within a couple of periods.

This was also a big day for me personally. The discovery of how powerful recognition can be changed how I work with my own team. Yes, I created change that day for the team through the standing ovations, but they also transformed me in profound new ways.

MADDY'S LEARNINGS

Standing ovations are too rare, and they can really change people. They make performance matter, and they feel good. People like to feel good, so figure out how to give standing ovations in your environment. I recommend that your standing ovations be loud foot stomping, cheering, and whistling events! Standing ovations create standing ovations!

Also, are C-Players really C-Players? They may simply be led by C-Leaders.

GAPOLOGY LESSONS
COMMUNICATION
ROOT SOLUTION

Importance Gaps are most often the result of the leader's lack of clear communication.

Just like recurring Knowledge Gaps imply a talent issue with a team member, recurring Importance Gaps imply a clarity and prioritization issue with the leader.

Winning leaders assume nothing. They over communicate a clear message and ensure it is understood. Winning leaders use communication as a tool to win and do not take it for granted. They carefully select the correct type of communication that will be most effective in delivering the desired result. Winning leaders leverage communication as a differentiator. It closes gaps. That is Gapology!

Clear, concise, and verified communication closes Importance Gaps.

Winning leaders only conduct meetings with a purpose and an objective, designed to create action in the team. They do not meet to just to meet.

Here are tactics that winning leaders use to turn meetings into action:

- Agenda
- Objective
- Random Recaps
- Calls to Action
- Post-meeting Assignments

Performance Gaps exist because of the lack of clear leadership. Winning leaders create winning followers.

We found certain "guideposts" winning leaders use to create a culture of followership:

- Mission Statement
- Organizational Values
- Leadership Competencies

The following eight competencies best capture those possessed by winning leaders and represent a strong force in closing Performance Gaps:

Gapology Top Eight Winning Leader Competencies:

- Embracing Change
- Managerial Courage
- Communicator
- Results-Driven
- Motivator
- Active Listener
- Responsible
- Competitive

You must structure your meetings to set action as an objective and not just a hopeful outcome.

Winning leaders use a "W" Meeting Structure to close the Importance Gap and move teams to action.

Standing ovations are too rare, and they can really change people. They make performance matter, and they feel good. Standing ovations create standing ovations!

10

PRIORITIZATION
ROOT SOLUTION

Whoever first said, "If everything is important, nothing is important." knew about Importance Gaps. One of keys to closing Importance Gaps is always keeping the team focused on the priorities, especially when they are shifting.

"Winning leaders create clear priorities using their actions and their words."

Prioritization is about decision-making. When you know what matters because the priorities are clear, decisions are easier to make.

Most gaps are caused by inaction. Clear priorities create action.

Priorities are not simply a list of stuff on a page. They are the things that people must do to achieve expectations. They are tied to a result component.

Leader behavior and actions must reflect the priorities. It really doesn't matter what the leader says or writes down. What matters most is what the leader does. Take for instance the leader who says that customer service is the number one priority for their team, but does not reinforce observed good service, ignores poor service, or even worse, does not personally model good customer service behavior when given the opportunity. This sends a confusing message to the team. The leader's behavior communicates the priorities to the team, whether intentional or not.

Winning leaders create clear priorities using their actions and their words. They keep the pathway to great decision making simple for their team. They empower the team within a framework and they set a great example. In this type of environment, decision-making is simple, priorities are clear, and productivity is high.

CREATING SHARED VISION

The "God's Child Project" helps educate, feed, clothe, and care for underprivileged children in Central America and Africa. It was founded by Patrick Atkinson and is directed by a board of true enduring heroes like, Pete Miller of Dallas, Texas. These people know how to create a shared vision.

Everyone we have met in this organization knows that the number-one priority is educating the kids. That overarching priority and shared vision built around breaking the shackles of poverty through education provides a clear benchmark for every decision made by every volunteer. It's all about educating kids so they can have a better life than their parents. God's Child even goes as far as building a home for the parents of kids who get good grades.

Clarity of priorities closes any potential Importance Gaps by creating a strong and compelling shared vision.

A trend in company teambuilding has emerged in recent years. Teams are participating in community events to build their own teamwork. Many teams tend to work in silos and don't effectively communicate or have a shared vision, but by working together to build a house or repaint classrooms at a local school, the walls of the silos begin to break down. The Gapology team has experienced this firsthand by working with Junior Achievement in Colorado to teach in seventh- and eighth-grade classrooms in challenged metro areas of Denver.

Events like this are a great way to truly make a difference in the community and build a stronger team with your coworkers.

This facilitates shared vision and causes the team to reflect on what matters most in their own lives. After a day of teaching, we conduct a debriefing session with the team and talk about what we will do differently and what commitments we will make for the upcoming year.

Creating a shared vision is significant because it creates a roadmap for closing Performance Gaps, specifically Importance and Action Gaps. For these gaps there is truly no greater way to align priorities than by creating a shared vision within your team.

Shared vision is about alignment of purpose. When a team has a shared vision, it operates as one. It is a powerful thing. You feel a bond with the team that you may not experience again during your lifetime. Teams with shared vision are unique; they are rare and hard to duplicate.

So how do you create a shared vision?

It is certainly one of the "arts" in closing Importance Gaps, and it is one of the most difficult things great leaders do. Many leaders do not inherently possess this skill, but it can be developed. It is one of those skills that call upon many other skills to become complete. Creating shared vision separates the winning leaders from the rest.

Here are the steps in creating a shared vision that we learned from winning leaders:

START WITH THE "WHY"

Explain the "why" behind your vision and expectations as a leader. Tell the team what you want to accomplish and what its role is. Tie the vision and expectations to a bigger purpose. Repeat your expectations every time you speak to your team. Make the things your team is working on bigger than life. People yearn to be part of something bigger than them. We see this over and over in nonprofit work. People view their lives as normal, but they see the purpose of the nonprofit as really important and life changing. The same is true for great teams bonded together for any winning cause.

MAKE AN INDIVIDUAL'S ROLE IMPORTANT

Help people see their critical role and how it ties to the big picture. Make their role and their performance important. Recognize them publicly. Many people never receive a standing ovation in their lifetime. Whenever you get your team together, give those individuals who deserve one a standing ovation. Let everyone know what you value by the behaviors and results you recognize.

KEEP THE VISION NARROW, BUT BIG

Go for big stuff! People can get excited about big things but not a list of things. More can be less. Shared vision is generally about one big thing. Look at our nation's history. As a country, we've rallied at different times around freedom, voters' rights, women's rights, equality for all people, and other vital causes.

MADDY'S STORY

THE THREE BIG FOCUSES

I want to share my "Three Big Focuses" tactic with you. It is simple and has served me very well, becoming foundational to my team's repetitive winning seasons. Here it is, but don't assume that it's as simple as it sounds. Priority creep is very easy to fall into. Three can become thirty without your gatekeeping leadership.

I keep myself and my team focused on only three focuses at a time. For each focus, there are well-defined and clearly measurable behavioral and result expectations. That's it, but don't underestimate its power.

Why is three the maximum number?

I have found three to be the magic number. It is not only significant enough to make great execution a reality, but it is also the number of expectations that can be successfully tackled at one time by a skilled leader and team.

My three focuses do not change much over the course of the year. What may change are the tactics within each of the focuses.

Through the successes within the focuses, we may learn tactics that we did not know when the year began, so it is important to apply any new tactics and stay flexible to shift tactics as the year progresses.

Every time I speak to my team, whether in a meeting, on a conference call, or when I meet with them in person, I speak about these "Three Big Focuses" and the expectations attached to each. I talk about how we are performing and ask the team to discuss the tactics they are using to execute the focuses.

Some might call this a narrow focus, and it is, but the "Three Big Focuses" are much more. They are important things tied to our overall financial goals. They are big enough that almost everything of importance fits within the focuses.

Less is more when it comes to the focuses of a high-performance team. The fewer things on which you are focused, the greater the focus on each.

MADDY'S LEARNINGS

Keep your team focused on three or fewer, measurable objectives and hold them accountable for great performance. This provides the team, and you, with clear, obtainable goals and expectations that, when performed at a high level, will allow you to join that exclusive club we call winning leaders.

GAPOLOGY LESSONS
PRIORITIZATION
ROOT SOLUTION

Whoever first said, "If everything is important, nothing is important" knew about Importance Gaps. One of keys to closing Importance Gaps is always keeping the team focused on the priorities, especially when they are shifting.

Prioritization is about decision-making. When you know what matters because the priorities are clear, decisions are easier to make.

Leader behavior and actions must reflect the priorities. It really doesn't matter what the leader says or writes down. What matters most is what the leader does.

Clarity of priorities closes any potential Importance Gaps by creating a strong and compelling shared vision.

Creating a shared vision is significant because it creates a roadmap for closing Performance Gaps, specifically Importance and Action Gaps. For these gaps, there is truly no greater way to align priorities than by creating a shared vision within your team.

Here are the steps in creating a shared vision that we learned from winning leaders:

- Start with the "why."
- Make an individual's role important.
- Keep the vision narrow, but big.

ACTION
GAP

PART 3

ACTION GAPS

11

IDENTIFYING ACTION GAPS

Action Gaps are the gaps between knowing the importance of an action and actually taking that action.

This is big.

What if a team member knows what to do, how to do it, and knows it is important, but still doesn't do it? Now that is a really big gap!

"Action Gaps in the behavior of leaders create much bigger gaps downstream."

This is where the rubber meets the road in Gapology, because it is all about the choice of the individual. Ultimately, he or she needs to make the choice to take action. This choice can be made consciously or subconsciously, but it is still a choice that is made or not made. Action or inaction…that is the question.

It may be the easiest gap to identify because it is the gap that is most obvious, but the Root Solutions are the most difficult.

Action Gaps are also the most costly gaps. They result in lost productivity, sales, and profits. They are the source of great frustration and stress for many leaders. The good news is that these gaps can be overcome. You've come to the right place. This is where you earn the title "Gapologist," and everything else in Gapology has been leading up to this.

Let's go back to our example of Maddy's team of ten sales managers. They are now in period three and once again have a sales plan of $5 million. You will recall that in each of the first two periods, Maddy's team was up against a sales plan of $5 million and missed plan by a combined $700,000.

Six of the ten sales managers made the sales plan in periods one and two by fully executing the three-step selling process. Upon further investigation, Maddy found that the four managers who missed their sales plan did not fully execute the three-step process.

Let's review the actions Maddy took at the end of period two:

- She brought the four sales managers who missed their sales plan together for a meeting and reviewed the three-step process. This was, in essence, an underperformers' or "gap" meeting.

- She accepted blame for not following up on their lack of execution.

- She discussed the success of the three-step process where it had been fully implemented and asked for their commitment to the process in the upcoming period.

- She gained their agreement and their timeline for role-playing and practicing the three-step process with any remaining sales reps who had not been covered.

- She asked what consequences there should be for any sales manager who fails to fully execute the three-step process. She agreed to the consequences the sales managers referenced.

- During the first week of period three, she attended a meeting with each of their sales rep teams to review and role-play the three-step process. She even participated in the role-play.

- She developed a weekly follow-up plan to ensure execution of the three-step process. Plus, she added a layer of business analysis to determine the outliers in sales, both good and bad, to understand the gaps.

The stage is finally set for a successful period. The plan for the period three is $5 million once again. The same three-step process is the clear ticket to achieving the sales plan.

Maddy's behavior as the leader has been much different this period. She is assuming almost nothing and verifying almost everything. Her follow-up is intense and relentless. The team has noticed, and the sales managers have commented to each other on the difference.

As the period progresses, it becomes clear that seven of the managers are fully executing the three steps and beating sales plan, but three still have Performance Gaps.

With a short call and some simple questions, Maddy verifies once again that these three sales managers have no Knowledge Gaps or Importance Gaps relating to the execution of the three-step process. They confirm knowledge of the process and assure Maddy that their entire sales rep team has knowledge and understands the importance of executing.

The Knowledge Gaps and Importance Gaps are closed! That leaves Action Gaps as the primary obstacle to performance. So is verifying that the Knowledge Gaps and Importance Gaps are closed sufficient?

As shown in Figure 13, period three ends, and Maddy's team has achieved the $5 million! She and the team have made the sales plan!

Congratulations, Maddy and team? Not so quick.

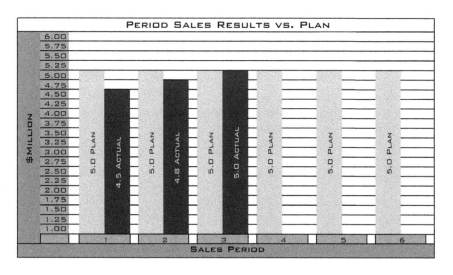

FIGURE 13 - PERIODS ONE THROUGH THREE SALES

Upon review of the period three sales results, Maddy sees that seven of the sales managers made their sales plan, and as a combined group these seven beat the sales plan by $500,000, but the three who were also noted as having Performance Gaps in period one and two missed the sales plan in period three by a combined total of $500,000. The C-Group offset the A-Group! Ouch. Maddy and team are still $700,000 under plan for the first three periods.

The three that missed plan were three of the four sales managers who had attended the "gap" meeting and had agreed to consequences for not fully executing the three-step process. They had also required Maddy's significant follow-up with themselves and their sales rep teams to even achieve their sub plan results.

Although she is proud of the overall team for achieving the $5 million plan, she realizes that if the three underperforming sales managers had made the plan, they would have produced $5.5 million and beat period three expectations by $500,000.

Because of her weekly follow-up and meetings with their teams, she is aware that these three did not fully execute the three-step process, and it appears to have cost Maddy's team $500,000 in sales. Maddy is careful not to react negatively toward the whole team, because the three-step process is now being executed by most of the reps, and the team overall made the sales plan. She congratulates the team, calls out the heroes, and makes everyone very clear on the power of the three-step process.

But, Maddy is clear that she is staring at a series of Action Gaps with three sales managers, and these have a $500,000 price tag! Ouch! She is upset, but contained and very resolved.

Winning isn't easy, and winning leaders take action to ensure victory.

Maddy had already changed her behavior as the leader from period one to two, then to three. She had successfully closed the Knowledge and Importance Gaps with her team through her intense follow-up, but now she had identified clear Action Gaps with three of her sales managers.

Action Gaps in the behavior of leaders are unacceptable to winning leaders because they know that these gaps create much bigger gaps downstream.

Although her team's performance improved in period three and achieved the sales plan, she was still not a winning leader. Her region manager informs her that if they had achieved $5.5 million, or $500,000 over the sales plan, Maddy's team would have been the top-performing district in the company.

Were the Action Gaps of the three sales managers acceptable? Absolutely not!

Would the gaps be closed for period four? Not likely, unless further action was taken.

These Action Gaps were very costly. To someone as competitive as Maddy, this is almost too much to bear, and these gaps are too costly for any company to accept. Her reputation and career were on the line. Maddy must take further action. Her whole team is watching. This is the essence of leadership.

Here are the Action Gaps Maddy identified in the three sales managers during period three:

- During her face-to-face follow-up meetings with the three sales managers, Maddy finds that all three have multiple sales reps that still have not successfully role-played and practiced the three-step process to the Habit Level. The three-step process is admittedly not being used with each customer on a consistent basis. This is despite the sales managers' commitment to close all Knowledge and Importance Gaps with the reps. This has left numerous sales reps vulnerable to missing sales. Not coincidentally, each of the sales reps identified, missed their sales plan in period three.

- Maddy also uncovered that the three sales managers each had significant Knowledge Gaps regarding the individual sales performances by rep. Sales by rep reporting should have been a key indicator as to whether the three-step process was in place or not.

We learned from winning leaders the steps to identify Action Gaps:

Winning Leader Behaviors to Identify Action Gaps

Review results and identify potential Performance Gaps.

Observe team behavior where result expectations are not being met while looking for gaps.

Inquire about key behavioral and result expectations and confirm understanding.

Declare the gaps.

Reset expectations and reiterate the consequences.

Follow up for immediate behavior and result changes.

PERFORMANCE BRIDGES ACTION TO RESULTS

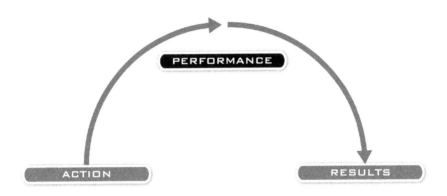

FIGURE 14 - PERFORMANCE BRIDGE MODEL

The simplicity of Figure 14 illustrates a very big concept.

Simply taking an action does not mean that it is the right action. There is a big difference between action and performance. When you get your team to take the right action, that action equals performance, and performance achieves the desired results. The C-Group tends to react and blame when the team misses expectations. This causes their teams to spin and often take the wrong action.

So, performance bridges action to results. This is how winning leaders consistently achieve and exceed result expectations.

Remember, "Busy ain't productive!"

Don't confuse being busy with being productive. Busy is action, but true productivity is performance (right action) that delivers desired results. Many people have simply learned to look productive.

Teams and organizations that do not keep score effectively may confuse the hard workers with the productive team members. In these organizations, there is no bridge from action to results.

Action can be busy work and may not equal performance. Desired results sit off in the distance as unachievable goals. One sign of an Action Gap is the tendency for the team to want to lower the bar when expectations are not met. If they are not meeting or exceeding expectations, the expectations must be too high, right? An example of the team's response might be, "We are working really hard, but the sales plans are really high!"

Blaming the sales plan is a sign of a low-productivity team and a sign of significant Action Gaps.

Imagine a pole vault team working toward a trip to the Olympics. Do they lower the bar to a level that everyone can comfortably get over? No. They keep raising the bar and challenging the team to achieve new heights.

Winning leaders keep their eye on the results and the behaviors that will achieve those results. When results are not being met, and the behaviors that equal performance are not in place, you have found a gap.

Bridging action to results with performance is the solution.

Begin completing your bridge by becoming aware of the power of performance and also by helping your teams become aware of its power.

Awareness is the first step toward action. Once the right action begins, winning is just around the corner!

KEY QUESTIONS WINNING LEADERS ASK THEIR TEAMS

- What behaviors are needed to achieve the expected results?
- What Action Gaps have you observed?
- Is the team committed to the behavior and the result expectations?
- How are you applying accountability for the behavior and result expectations?

GAPOLOGY LESSONS
IDENTIFYING ACTION GAPS

Action Gaps are the gaps between knowing the importance of an action and actually taking that action.

This is where the rubber meets the road in Gapology, because it is all about the choice of the individual. Ultimately, he or she needs to make the choice to take action.

It may be the easiest gap to identify because it is the gap that is most obvious, but the Root Solutions are the most difficult.

Action Gaps in the behavior of leaders are unacceptable to winning leaders, because they know that these gaps create much bigger gaps downstream.

Winning Leader Behaviors to Identify Action Gaps

- *Review results and identify potential Performance Gaps.*
- *Observe team behavior where result expectations are not being met while looking for gaps.*
- *Inquire about key behavioral and result expectations and confirm understanding.*
- *Declare the gaps.*
- *Reset expectations and reiterate the consequences.*
- *Follow up for immediate behavior and result changes.*

Performance bridges action to results. This is how winning leaders consistently achieve and exceed result expectations.

When you get your team to take the right action, that action equals performance, and performance achieves the desired results.

Winning leaders keep their eye on the results and the behaviors that will achieve those results. When results are not being met, and the behaviors that equal performance are not in place, you have found a gap.

159

12

CLOSING
ACTION GAPS

The gap between performing to expectations and not performing to expectations can be subtle and hidden from a casual glance. Winning leaders do not take a casual glance.

In this case, there is no question as to which gaps Maddy has identified. She has significant Action Gaps with three key leaders. This clarity has come through her methodical use of Gapology and through the closure of Knowledge and Importance Gaps.

"Closing the gaps in sequential order (Knowledge, Importance, and then Action) creates the foundation for great performance."

As discussed earlier, the C-Leaders will tend to react in situations like this by blaming the whole team for the sales miss. This creates more gaps. The team that made sales plan is getting blamed, too? You can see how that would be confusing and demoralizing, too.

Like a skilled surgeon, Maddy has isolated the issues so each can be dealt with. She has also closed the Knowledge and Importance Gaps, so they can't be reopened. She now operates from a position of strength, having learned from her mistakes, seeing clearly that her behavior was a big part of the issue in periods one and two, but no more. She knows what she must do to close the Action Gaps in her team.

Here are the steps Maddy takes to close the Action Gaps to ensure the team exceeds the sales plan in period four and gets back on track for the year:

- In the week following the close of period three, Maddy schedules each of the three sales managers who missed the sales plan for an individual face-to-face meeting in her office. She schedules them one hour apart, so they see each other as they come and go. This will ensure that word of the face-to-face meetings spreads throughout the team, reinforcing Maddy's commitment to the three-step process. This further tightens the seal on Importance Gaps.

- Each of the three sales managers is instructed to bring a written plan addressing how they will achieve their sales plan in period four and make up any year-to-date deficit by the end of period six.

- As she meets with each, Maddy expresses her disappointment in his or her results and behavior. She asks each to explain his or her Performance Gaps, confirming that the Knowledge and Importance Gaps are closed. She does not reference the three-step process in the communication and instruction on the development of a written plan. She needs to test their ownership for the three-step process.

- Maddy outlines the consequences for missing the sales plan in period four and for any further Action Gaps. She asks questions to verify their understanding and documents their commitments, giving them a copy and placing a copy in the sales manager's personnel file.

- She allows them to briefly present their plans and asks follow-up questions. She asks for their commitment to the plan to achieve the period four sales goal and make up the sales deficit by period six.

- Maddy schedules time during week two of period four to meet with each of the three sales managers and their sales rep teams to observe team behavior and review results. This gives them enough time to make significant progress in closing gaps in their performance.

Action Gaps are the most difficult to close because the final ownership of taking action is now in the hands of the team. You have closed the Knowledge Gaps and the Importance Gaps, and now your team is set to effectively close the Action Gaps.

We learned from winning leaders the steps to close Action Gaps:

Winning Leader Behaviors to Close Action Gaps

Declare the Action Gap.

Inquire about expectations.

Repeat expectations.

Create accountability.

Manage the gaps in performance.

Apply recognition and consequences.

Do you think Maddy's team has closed the Action Gaps?

At this point, she has placed the responsibility in the hands of the three sales managers. She has begun creating a culture of action, and they must take the required action. Behavior change in the three sales managers needs to be immediate. Maddy has done her part, but it is up to the three sales managers to fully execute the three-step process, get their rep teams up to speed, and achieve the sales plan.

The face-to-face meetings with each of the three sales managers worked! By closing their Action Gaps, all three made the plan in period four, pushing Maddy's team to a victorious $5.5 million, or $500,000 over plan.

As shown in Figure 15, period four sales were $1 million more than were produced in period one:

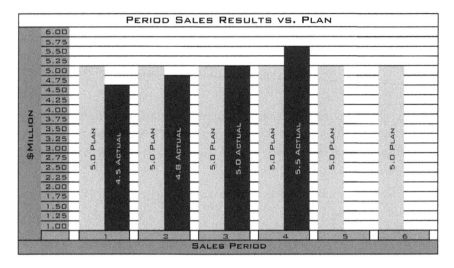

FIGURE 15 - PERIODS ONE THROUGH FOUR SALES

Figure 16 shows that Maddy's team repeated their winning behaviors in the remaining months of the year, and Maddy achieved her first of three consecutive "District Manager of the Year" awards. What could have been a losing year after three very rough periods and a sizable year-to-date deficit became a winning season! Maddy's focus on closing the Performance Gaps with her team was the key.

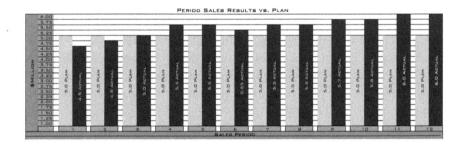

FIGURE 16 - FULL YEAR SALES

Winning leaders never give up! They stay focused on closing gaps! Closing the gaps in sequential order (Knowledge, Importance, and then Action) creates the foundation for great performance and results. Maddy used Gapology to build a winning team, a winning season, and a winning career, and her passion for Gapology spread like wildfire throughout XYZ.

GAPOLOGY LESSONS
CLOSING ACTION GAPS

Action Gaps are the most difficult to close because the final ownership of taking action is now in the hands of the team. You have closed the Knowledge Gaps and the Importance Gaps, and now your team is set to effectively close the Action Gaps.

Winning Leader Behaviors to Close Action Gaps

- *Declare the Action Gap.*
- *Inquire about expectations.*
- *Repeat expectations.*
- *Create accountability.*
- *Manage the gaps in performance.*
- *Apply recognition and consequences.*

Winning leaders never give up! They stay focused on closing gaps! Closing the gaps in sequential order (Knowledge, Importance, and then Action) creates the foundation for great performance and results.

13

ACCOUNTABILITY
ROOT SOLUTION

Winning leaders create accountability using a variety of different methods, but the old-fashioned way still works best.

They set clear expectations and follow up.

We know that this may sound too simple, but it works even though many leaders dramatically underutilize it. If you are good at this one thing, it will make the other elements of successfully leading teams easier.

"Winning leaders create accountability by transferring ownership of their own plays to others."

Creating accountability is a skill that can be learned, so get good at it!

Here are the four winning leader tactics to create accountability:

SET EXPECTATIONS

Winning leaders are clear on the behavior and result expectations. They follow up and create accountability around these. In addition to what they expect, they are clear on when things must be done. To ensure understanding and alignment, they have the team member repeat back the expectations and the timeframes. As we have already reviewed, setting expectations is not only a Root Solution to closing Importance Gaps, but it also creates accountability.

FOLLOW-UP

Winning leaders follow up in a timely manner, and by doing so they teach their teams that they will follow up again next time. This conditions the behavior of the team to respond and get ahead of the leaders' follow-up. Timely follow-up is important. Laying out the specific follow-up timeframes and methods is crucial. For example, you might say, "I expect a call on Friday at 2:00 pm for you to update me on the status of the project." This closes Action Gaps quickly, if the leader is consistent.

KEEP SCORE

Winning leaders keep score! As we have already reviewed, keeping score not only closes Importance Gaps, but it also creates action and therefore closes Action Gaps. Set result expectations; publish important metrics using green, red, and yellow highlights; and create a focus around areas or individuals where results significantly exceed or miss the expectations. All of these are effective in creating action. Keeping score motivates people to perform better. It ignites an internal fire and is a game-changer.

TRANSFER OWNERSHIP

Winning leaders close the Knowledge and Importance Gaps by transferring ownership for the action to the team member. This positions the leader to effectively coach the team member to achieve the desired outcome. In an environment where ownership is transferred, there is less need for the traditional reward and penalty structure. Teams that know the expectations will own the responsibility of meeting them and perform at a higher level.

Team members on a team know who is performing and who is not performing. They watch to see how the leader creates accountability. Like setting expectations, setting consequences is critical. Winning teams, given clarity of expectations and consequences, will self-manage underperformers off the team. They take pride in their team's performance and results. Anyone who stands in the way is not welcome. C-Players, as discussed in the Root Solution-Talent chapter, prefer to be surrounded with C-Players, so they will often self-select off of a winning team.

Winning leaders create accountability and a sense of ownership in others.

As we discussed earlier, the quarterback of a football team owns the ball once it is hiked into his hands, until he has securely handed it off to the running back. The ownership for that play has now been transferred to the running back, and the eventual outcome of the play is now in the hands of the running back.

Winning leaders create accountability by transferring ownership of their own plays to others.

WINNING LEADERS HAVE "EDGE"

Winning leaders use EDGE to create action and accountability. As displayed in Figure 17, EDGE Model, the acronym of EDGE lays out the key elements that they consistently apply in their drive to win. EDGE is: Energy, Decisive, Greatness, and Expectations.

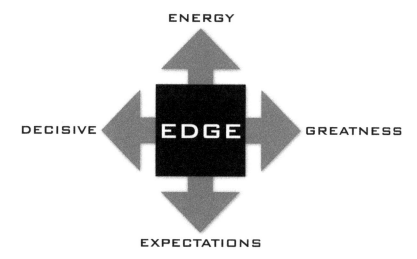

FIGURE 17 - EDGE MODEL

EDGE can be described as a strong point of view or belief in something. It is being unwavering and showing unwillingness to compromise on values and standards. It is not mean spirited. It brings others along because it is inspirational. EDGE is found in the winning leader's passion about that belief. It can be heard in how they speak. We developed the acronym to best fit the elements winning leaders bring to the game. They display and create Energy. They are Decisive. Greatness is their standard. Expectations are a tool they use to drive performance. So, EDGE fits winning leaders.

Here are the detailed descriptions of EDGE:

ENERGY

Energy displayed by speaking with passion about key actions then creates energy in others. Others will act because of the leader's energy. The energy behind the things they say shows they believe them to the core. This brings others along and causes them to sign on to the vision. Winning leaders display EDGE with energy when they describe their vision. They speak and act with energy to create followers. Don't confuse this energy with charisma. Not all winning leaders have charisma.

DECISIVE

Decisive means having a point of view and not hesitating to make the decisions that are right for the organization and its values. Winning leaders are decisive and set the example for their teams. They display managerial courage and do not fear decisions. Instead, they are empowered by the decision-making process. It comes with the territory. Winning leaders are predictable. You always know where they are coming from. This allows their teams to be decisive as well. These leaders are not swayed by the political winds. When leaders waste an inordinate amount of time reviewing everyone's opinion, they are not being decisive and have lost their EDGE. Winning leaders are direct and do not hesitate to give constructive feedback to the team.

GREATNESS

Greatness is an expectation set forth by winning leaders both for themselves and their teams. Is greatness in performance and results something you expect? If not, do you expect mediocrity? There is no middle ground. As Jim Collins said in the opening line of his bestselling book *Good to Great*, "Good is the enemy of great." Why? If you settle for good, great will happen only by chance. The pursuit of greatness is inspiring, and it's a big thing that others will buy into and want to be a part of. Greatness is not easy, and not everyone will want to come along. Collins could also have added that mediocre is the enemy of good, and pathetic is the enemy of mediocre. Why get out of bed in the morning if the bar is set at mediocre or even good levels? It is just not enough. A-Players, as we discussed earlier in the book, have an expectation of greatness for themselves, their supervisor, their peers, and their team. They play to win. Winning leaders set an expectation of greatness and do so with EDGE. This moves their teams to action.

EXPECTATIONS

Expectations are delivered with an EDGE. Winning leaders set expectations for their teams with this passionate EDGE. If you take out the EDGE, expectations really aren't expectations. They simply become goals. Expectations are not aspirational. They are nonnegotiable! Setting expectations with EDGE takes practice. Most leaders struggle to set clear expectations. Work at it. This is one of the biggest differences between winning leaders and those who settle for just being "good."

PROGRESS VERSUS MEETING EXPECTATIONS

Progress is good, but celebrating it may inhibit achieving the expectations.

Hold your team accountable for achieving the expectations versus over celebrating their progress. Have you ever set expectations for your team only to see them improve but never actually achieved the expectations?

A winning leader taught us the analogy that progress is like driving a car down a long highway and looking in the rearview mirror to see how far you have come. Expectations, where you are going, are not visible in the rearview mirror. They are out ahead of you through the windshield. Expectations can only be achieved by looking forward and keeping your eyes on the road as you move to the destination you desire. It may be helpful to be conscious of where you are currently and look back occasionally to learn from the potholes and bumps you've experienced along the way, and you can course-correct by applying those learnings. If you keep your eyes on the rearview mirror, however, you may not see the new obstacles in front of you and will most likely crash.

So, acknowledge your team's progress, but keep them focused on achieving the expectations. Progress can give leaders the false perception that the team will meet the expectations soon. Oftentimes, teams fall backward after progress, reverting to old behaviors, but winning leaders keep the expectations clear and are not satisfied with mere progress.

WINNING LEADERS KEEP SCORE

Winning leaders keep score. This became very clear to us during the interviews we conducted with leaders. Winning leaders, without exception, were connected to the key metrics of performance. They communicated the performance metrics to their team daily, weekly, each period, and often throughout the day. Winning leaders break down the metrics by team member to make the metrics real and meaningful. They also tie metrics to behavior. The C-GROUP, by contrast, was much less connected to metrics. Their teams were less aware of key metrics, and often they were totally unaware of how the team was performing or how they were performing personally. One of the scariest characteristics we found in the C-Group teams was their view that their performance was "good," when the metrics suggested otherwise.

No matter what you do, there are ways to keep score, and the act of keeping score impacts behavior. Creating a culture that keeps score creates a culture of action. What you score becomes important, so the leader must carefully narrow the metrics to those that matter most.

A word of caution, however: if you score everything, people will simply gravitate to the things that they do well and suggest that this implies that they are performing. If you score everything, you will not have a successful team, and you will confuse your team. What you score matters. We found that three to five key metrics is the most effective number to focus upon.

MADDY'S STORY
BORROWING POWER

I visited with an underperforming sales manager to try to understand the reasons for his poor results. Rob was a new sales manager and seemed to have all of the right ingredients for success, but he could not consistently meet expectations. I decided to observe his interactions with his team and just take notes on how he led. I intended to record Rob's behaviors that were positive and those that might be at the root of his missing expectations.

During this process, I actually scribed what Rob said to his team. I have found this to be a helpful tactic when I review my findings with the leader. You may want to bring tape to cover your mouth if you are anything like me. It is very tempting to jump into the conversation with the team and correct their flaws right on the spot. Unfortunately, this stifles their learning and isn't helpful.

I observed Rob and his team for two days. During this time, he held a conference call with his entire team, and he visited with two different sales reps and coached their performance. You would have been proud of me, or at least I was proud of myself. I kept quiet and took notes. I also found the issue. Rob borrowed power. He borrowed my power, and I have found that leaders who borrow their boss's power never create their own. As a result, they fail.

Let me explain how borrowing power results in failure. Rob mentioned my name in the two days, either directly or by implication, twenty-seven times. Everything was about me, his supervisor. The reason that we must do something was always about me. It was never about being in the best interest of the customer. It was never explained with EDGE as Rob's expectation. It was always about my expectations and me. He was borrowing power. He had become a traffic cop sent to enforce my expectations. He was not the sales manager, and he was not leading. He did not believe in what we were doing, and it was evident to everyone.

Here are some examples of what Rob said to his team:

> "Maddy expects us to execute the three-step selling process."
> "She won't settle for less than excellence."
> "You are going to get me in big trouble with my boss."

So what damaging message was Rob sending to the team?

Let's list some of the most likely possibilities:

- Rob did not own the expectations of our team and, therefore, did not create expectations with his team.
- Rob did not share the vision. He did not believe in the vision. It was my vision, not his. He was just an enforcer.
- Rob did not transfer ownership to the sales reps and did not hold them accountable.
- At the end of the second day, when I sat down and reviewed my observations with Rob, he was taken by surprise. He had assumed that since I had not offered any input for two grueling days, everything was fine.

When I asked him how many times he had used my name, he could only remember a few. That is why the note-taking process is so critical.

I asked Rob about using my name and how he felt that it reflected on him and his authority. I spoke to him about borrowing power and the damage it may do to his team, specifically in the areas of setting expectations and creating accountability.

Most of my stories have had a happy ending. This one does not. Rob did not change his behavior despite this exercise and a few other similar visits. He continued to borrow power while failing to hold his team accountable, and, as a result, I was forced to replace him.

The good news is that Rob was the only direct report of mine who did not respond positively to coaching on this topic. Coaching on "borrowing power" generally works and leads to improved performance.

MADDY'S LEARNINGS

Winning leaders transfer ownership for expectations to the individual who is responsible for the performance. As a leader, you must own their expectations as well. You must never borrow the power of your boss or a higher authority to get something done. Borrowing power signals a lack of buy-in to the vision and a lack of leadership. It may also imply a lack of managerial courage and EDGE.

GAPOLOGY LESSONS
ACCOUNTABILITY
ROOT SOLUTIONS

Winning leaders create accountability. They use a variety of different ways to do this, but the old-fashioned way still works best. They simply set clear expectations and follow up.

Here are the four winning leader tactics to create accountability:

- *Set Expectations*
- *Follow Up*
- *Keep Score*
- *Transfer Ownership*

Winning leaders use EDGE to create action and accountability.

EDGE is:

- Energy
- Decisive
- Greatness
- Expectations

Progress is good, but celebrating it may inhibit achieving the expectations.

Hold your team accountable for achieving the expectations versus over celebrating their progress.

A winning leader taught us the analogy that progress is like driving a car down a long highway and looking in the rearview mirror to see how far you have come. Expectations, where you are going, are not visible in the rearview mirror.

ACTION
GAP

ACCOUNTABILITY

COMMITMENT

CULTURE

14

COMMITMENT
ROOT SOLUTION

One extremely powerful tool that you can use to contrast the commitment and compliance levels of your team is the Commitment Ladder, Figure 18.

This can be very useful in determining and charting where your team falls on the continuum from non-compliance to commitment. As you evaluate your team, remember that their commitment level is topic-specific. Someone can be committed to selling or building relationships, but non-compliant when it comes to operations and administration. If the job requires all of these elements, this is a big problem.

"Team members who are committed or genuinely compliant to the vision will have fewer Action Gaps."

We have found it helpful for leaders to measure the team's level of commitment or compliance toward the overall mission and expectations of the organization. When coaching them, however, you could look at specific areas as examples to reference.

Leaders and team members who are committed or genuinely compliant to the vision of an organization will have fewer Action Gaps and will likely close them before they happen.

COMMITMENT LADDER

FIGURE 18 - COMMITMENT LADDER

Here are the definitions and coaching recommendations we use for each level:

NON-COMPLIANT

She is a performance issue. Quickly close any Knowledge and Importance Gaps, but do not accept non-compliance. Like the grudgingly compliant person, the non-compliant person stands out, and the rest of the team observes your leadership in handling this scenario. Your belief in the vision is under a microscope and will be questioned if you allow non-compliant behavior. If you hired this person, retool the interview and selection process. Set expectations and follow up multiple times per week if needed. Demand immediate compliance and be clear but swift on the consequences.

GRUDGINGLY COMPLIANT

He does what he needs to do to keep his job. He will often voice his true feelings to others but tell you what he thinks you want to hear. He does not believe in the vision. His behavior and lack of results show his lack of compliance. He can't be trusted and will need to become compliant to keep his seat on the bus. His grudging compliance is damaging to the team. It can be a cancer, and his peer group sees it and may view it as weakness in your leadership. He will cut corners. Set expectations and follow up often. He will not appreciate the oversight, but it is required because he will lower the productivity of the team.

FORMALLY COMPLIANT

She is a good soldier. She waits for direction and then executes effectively. She wants to fully implement the vision but has her hands full. She may be new in her position and not fully developed in her role. Her formal compliance needs to move to genuine compliance over time, especially if she leads others or works without direct supervision.

GENUINELY COMPLIANT

He has fully bought into the vision. He can be counted on to deliver a steady performance and is a good mentor to others. He executes the organization's business plan fully and takes pride in his work. Others will follow him, and he is considered a good leader. He is likely a B-PLAYER on your forced ranking. Let him help underperformers deliver the basics. This is the level you want to work to bring the team to. This level delivers a high level of performance. Remember, the "committed" team member is rare. Genuine compliance is to be applauded.

COMMITTED

She writes the rulebook. As a leader, you turn to her to take the lead. She influences the entire team and impacts results one level up from her position. She is the "go-to person" on the topic. Her commitment is obvious to all. She champions the organization's vision. She is often considered an A-PLAYER. Her passion is contagious. When she needs help, she reaches out to others, leaving her ego at the door. Challenge her with special projects and keep her in the spotlight. She wants your job. Leverage her commitment to impact the team's performance.

Charting your team's level of commitment is important and, as mentioned, should be applied independently to any significant initiative. Once charted, use the information to directly impact your leader behaviors. Winning leaders know that committed team members need to be treated differently than compliant team members. Each level has its own unique nuances and requires varied levels of direction and support, as does each individual person on the team.

If the direction and support is not appropriately applied, committed team members can slide down the Commitment Ladder, landing somewhere around the Grudgingly Compliant level. An example of this would be micromanaging someone who is committed. He or she may feel unvalued. Many grudgingly compliant team members are at that level as a direct reflection of the leader not being aware of their needs.

Winning leaders know their team!

There are many things that generate commitment within an individual. Managing unequally is key. Commitment comes from within, but the leader can help light the fire. Using the Root Solutions from this book will also help to do that most effectively. Train, teach, and fill your team with talent. Set clear expectations using strong communication around the highest priorities. Establish methods of accountability, stay committed yourself to the people on your team and the company's mission, goals, and expectations. Finally, create a culture of action for your team. These Root Solutions can fix almost any commitment issue you encounter as a leader when the Performance Gaps are identified quickly and accurately.

Included at the end of this chapter is an exercise where you will chart your team on the Commitment Ladder to help with diagnosing Performance Gaps. This is not something you would share openly with your team, but it will help you develop a course of action to improve your team's performance.

THE COMMITMENT LADDER

When I was first introduced to the Commitment Ladder, I knew I had found the secret to being a great leader. It is an amazing tool that allows me to "size up" my team, my peers, candidates for employment, and so on. I used to just base commitment on my gut feeling, but with the Commitment Ladder, I had a way to measure commitment.

And yes, I admit it. I measure the commitment of the people I surround myself with. It matters to me. I play to win, and that means my team must play to win, too.

I have found that some people are not committed to anything. That won't work for me. But if they are committed to something, then they are likely to become committed to the compelling vision I have. A lack of commitment is a sign of a mediocre life and a mediocre future. I like to align with people who are going after something, almost anything, because it tells me about a fire lit inside a person.

Here is an example. When I interviewed Alex, she was pretty unimpressive. She seemed to have low self-esteem and dressed sloppily. Her hair was messed up, and she talked just like she looked, until...

The interview was going so poorly that I shifted gears and asked Alex what she liked to do outside of work. She lit up like a Christmas tree. Her facial expressions changed, her posture jumped upright, the tone in her voice was suddenly upbeat, and so went my engagement.

Alex ran marathons. She was currently running twelve miles four time a week. Her diet had been adjusted to match her training regimen. She worked out five days a week on top of the running. I was sore just listening to her description. She had her eyes set on the top three marathons that summer.

She was committed to something.

I asked her about the impact of marathon training on her training to be a top sales manager. She was confused. I asked again about how she merged the trainings to be both a great marathon runner and sales manager. She had not considered taking a similar approach.

Alex was a project, but she was committed to something. I hired her despite of the shortcomings. Her training focused additional time on "vision" and becoming best in class. I worked with Alex to develop a training regimen for work that mirrored her marathon training.

Alex became a top performer. She leveraged her commitment to marathon running into a commitment to being a marathon-running sales manager.

MADDY'S LEARNINGS

Look for commitment in others. It tells you a lot about a person. Most people never achieve commitment to anything in their lives, so finding a "marathon runner" commitment level is a big deal. It takes an exceptional level of commitment to run marathons, just as it takes an exceptional level of commitment to be a great sales manager.

GAPOLOGY LESSONS
COMMITMENT
ROOT SOLUTION

One extremely powerful tool that you can use to contrast commitment and compliance levels on your team is the Commitment Ladder.

Leaders and team members who are committed or genuinely compliant to the vision of an organization will have fewer Action Gaps and will likely close them before they happen.

Commitment Ladder:

- Non-Compliant
- Grudgingly Compliant
- Formally Compliant
- Genuinely Compliant
- Committed

Charting your team's level of commitment is important and, as mentioned, should be applied independently to any significant initiative. Once charted, use the information to directly impact your leader behaviors. Winning leaders know that committed team members need to be treated differently than compliant team members.

Winning leaders know their team!

15

CULTURE
ROOT SOLUTION

A culture of action is the desired model for every organization. Imagine a team so closely aligned with the vision of the organization that everyone acts without being told.

But how do you get there?

How do you, as a leader, create an environment where action is automatic and inaction is the exception?

"If you do not have the desired culture in your organization, you need a change in the mindset of leadership."

We try to answer these and similar questions in this chapter by demonstrating how you can create a culture of action. Winning leaders do this consistently, seamlessly, so we felt it was critical to address this topic.

Gapology is a roadmap for changing an organization by changing the behavior of the organization. At the heart of this change is a change in mindset. Mindset is the launching pad for behavioral change.

A shift in the mindset of the leader creates lasting behavior change within a team. If you do not have the desired culture in your organization, you need a change in the mindset of leadership. It is about your mindset. Behavioral change needs to be intentional, and it is the catalyst to transforming an organization into something that it is not today.

BEING LADDER

One method of measuring the mindset level of team members and leaders is by identifying if they are at the Knowing, Doing, or Being Levels. When the leader is at a Being Level, the team shifts toward Being Level as well. They have no choice. This shifting of mindset becomes the true catalyst for behavioral change that will launch an organization into what we call a culture of action.

The Being Ladder shown in Figure 19 can be used to measure the level of a team's mindset and engagement to any specific initiative or even an organization's vision. Moving a team from the Doing Level to the Being Level in mindset is a critical component of success.

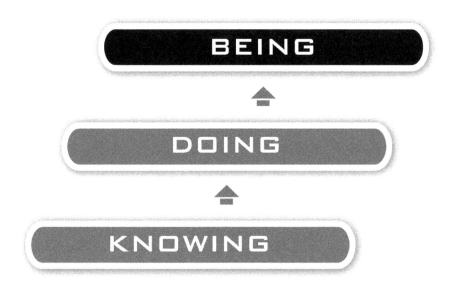

FIGURE 19 - BEING LADDER

Leaders in key positions must achieve Being Level mindset for great success to take hold and become a cultural. At the Being Level, Action Gaps are proactively closed and even prevented.

Winning leaders live at the Being Level in the important things.

Let's use Maddy's team and the three-step selling process to explain the engagement level that fits Knowing, Doing, and Being.

KNOWING

Sales managers and sales reps know the three-step selling process and can speak to it. They can describe, but not necessarily demonstrate, each of the three steps. At this level, there is great risk of inaction, because there is a big gap between knowing the three-step process and actually doing it with every customer. This mindset is below the level required for action to occur.

DOING

Sales managers and sales reps consistently model the three-step selling process in their interactions with customers. They believe in it and see its value. They know that executing the three-step process equals making the sales plan. This becomes the target level of mindset for most positions regarding any initiative because this means action, the right action, will be taken.

There is a risk here for leaders who Know, but don't Do. That is why it was critical for Maddy and the sales manager team to actually Do the three-step process. If they limit their mindset to Know the initiative will generally have lower value in the team's eyes. Leaders need to pick and choose which initiatives require that they step up beyond the level of Knowing.

BEING

Sales managers and sales reps teach and model the three-step selling process with new reps and managers. They give feedback and set a high expectation for execution of the process. They are the champions of the process and scale it forward without compromise to fit the presentation of new product lines. They create rules to support the process and measures to articulate its effectiveness. They believe in the process so much that they would continue the three-step process even if it were no longer a requirement of Maddy's. Their mindset is off the charts and evident to all. This level of mindset is aspirational. At the Being Level, leaders can move mountains and accomplish virtually anything. Their passion is contagious and brings others along.

As you can see, there is a huge difference between Knowing, Doing, and Being. As you look at your own team's behavior and execution of specific initiatives, ask yourself where they fall on this scale.

What is your expectation for mindset by position? Is it Knowing, Doing or Being?" Should you share that expectation with them and describe its meaning? Winning leaders move their teams to Doing and Being.

In Maddy's case, the three-step selling process has proven to be extremely effective, but the result would not have been reached without the great performance of the sales managers who designed it, combined with Maddy's full support and Being Level behavior. This is exactly why many program rollouts are not successful.

Thus, the buy-in of the leader behaving at the Being Level is paramount to an effective launch and ongoing performance. Winning leaders know this and use it to their advantage.

Team members know that programs will come and go. They just need to "wait it out and this one will pass, too." They know that in many cases, leaders appear supportive at the beginning of a launch but will wane as time goes by. But when confronted by a leader at the Being Level, they are more likely to buy in and work toward the Being Level themselves. It is a game-changer that winning leaders use to create great performance.

At the Being Level, you possess an internal fire about something that is clearly visible to the world around you. People will follow this fire, and that is why people follow winning leaders.

Don't confuse Doing with Being, as there is no comparison. A hiker at Being Level is standing on one side of the Grand Canyon looking back to the other side at another hiker who is at the Doing Level. They are not remotely close. They are separated by the great expanse of the Grand Canyon. Getting to the other side is no small feat. Being Level of engagement is no small feat either.

As a leader, you must choose Being Level to become a winning leader. You must choose to take that hike down into the canyon, cross the river, and hike up the other side.

Here are some things you must consider to become a winning leader and create a winning organization:

- What programs or processes are critical to the success of your organization?

- Where does your engagement fall, Knowing, Doing, or Being Level, in relation to these programs?

- If you say Being, would your team agree? Do they see Being Level when they look at your behavior?

Remember that a Being Level behavior is evident to everyone. Winning leaders shine because this moves others to the Being Level, and that creates great performance.

Next is an amazing and potentially game changing exercise for you to complete. We have had such success with this one that we wish we could be there with you when you try it. The exercise has you declare the mindset level by individual for a specific project or event. It is a great exercise and can be very eye opening.

KNOWING-DOING-BEING EXERCISE	
Business Case:	The BEING LADDER assesses a team's mindset level toward specific projects or events. It is a critical component to the project/event's success.
Items Needed:	Paper/flipchart/dry erase board with markers Direct report listing
1	Choose a specific current project or event that requires a team's high level of mindset.
2	Assess the team member's current level of mindset. (On the Being Ladder)
3	Coach the team to the expected level of mindset.
4	On future events, set an expected level of mindset and coach to it prior to the event kickoff.
5	Continue to engage all critical events before, during, and after to determine results and to make adjustments.

Example from Maddy's Team:

PROJECT/EVENT					Three-Step Selling Process				

	KNOWING				DOING			BEING		
	1	2	3	4	5	6	7	8	9	10
Michael										x
Emma									x	
Jamaal								x		
Aliya							x			
Javier						x				
Sara					x					
Isaac				x						
Li			x							
Susan		x								
Lucia	x									

Your turn to complete:

PROJECT/EVENT									

	KNOWING				DOING			BEING		
	1	2	3	4	5	6	7	8	9	10

TALENT, MINDSET, AND PERFORMANCE

We use an equation to predict the performance of an individual or a team. It has proven quite effective and quite accurate.

The equation is $T \times M = P$ as shown in Figure 20.

T is for Talent, M is for Mindset or state of mind, and P is for Performance.

So, Talent (0-10) multiplied by Mindset (0-10) equals Performance Level (0-100). Interesting! This means that Talent and Mindset are equal in determining performance. We have found that no matter how talented an individual, their Mindset Level plays an equal role in their Performance over time. The individual's work/life balance, job satisfaction, issues at home, etc. can all impact Mindset and can be as important as their Talent Level!

FIGURE 20 - T X M = P MODEL

An example would be as follows. Let's say you hire a talented team member who has a Talent Level of 8 out of 10. You are estimating this, of course. They love their new job and have always wanted that position, so their Mindset Level is high, and you rate it 9 out of 10. Their Performance level would then be 72 out of a possible 100. That is a very high number. You can expect great things!

Talent (8) x Mindset (9) = 72/100

Now, over time, you work to develop them in their role. Their Talent Level after one year has risen to 9, and their Mindset has remained high at 9. Their Performance is therefore likely to improve. They have moved from a Performance index of 72 up to 81, or greater than a 10 percent move. Fantastic!

Talent (9) x Mindset (9) = 81/100

Whether you are evaluating your current team or interviewing candidates for open positions, T x M = P, is a very helpful way to view current and future performance levels. Think about how this ties directly to the Commitment Ladder, which we revealed as part of the Importance Gap discussion.

All leaders have a significant impact on Mindset. We can't forget that. Winning leaders work hard to have a positive impact on the mindset of their team. Leaders impact talent through skill development, and if we also have a positive impact on Mindset we can help individuals reach their full potential. Winning leaders excel at developing the skills and increasing the Talent of their team.

The true value of a leader is fully expressed in the T and the M and therefore the P of their team. Winning leaders have teams with consistently higher P, and they therefore also have consistently higher results.

Also, keep in touch with your own T and M. When you are feeling down, your M plummets and therefore so does your P. You must control this because it impacts your team. When your M is low, it lowers the M of your team, too! Ensure that you are always raising your T by reading books, going to leadership conferences, etc. As your T goes up, you will the raise the T of your team.

The following T x M = P exercise is based on Maddy's experience. Review her team's rankings and the actions she utilized to improve her team, and then use the blank sections as a sample to complete with your own team.

T x M = P EXERCISE

Business Case:	T x M = P will give you an edge as you make decisions that impact your team. As a leader, you play a significant role in identifying and improving performance.
Items Needed:	Paper/flipchart/dry erase board with markers Direct report listing Leadership Ranking from "Play Chess, not Checkers" exercise (optional)
Steps:	
1	List each direct report on the chart. You may want to list in leadership rank order.
2	On a scale of 1-10 (1 being low and 10 being high) estimate and list their Talent levels.
3	On a scale of 1-10 (1 being low and 10 being high) estimate their Mindset levels.
4	Multiply the two level numbers to determine their Performance Predictor.
5	Develop actions to improve their Talent or Mindset levels.
6	Consider T x M = P when making decisions that impact your team members (e.g., relocations, realignments, etc.).

EXAMPLE FROM MADDY'S TEAM

Talent	
Michael	9
Emma	7
Jamaal	7
Aliya	6
Javier	8
Sara	9
Isaac	7
Li	6
Matt	5
Lucia	4

Mindset	
Michael	8
Emma	9
Jamaal	7
Aliya	6
Javier	6
Sara	5
Isaac	7
Li	5
Matt	5
Lucia	5

Performance Predictor	
Michael	72
Emma	63
Jamaal	49
Aliya	36
Javier	48
Sara	45
Isaac	49
Li	30
Matt	25
Lucia	20

	Actions to Improve Talent	Actions to Improve Mindset
Michael	Attend Gapology Seminar	Assign Special Project
Emma	Attend Gapology Seminar	Relocate Closer to Home
Jamaal	Read Gapology Book	Provide Additional Sales Rep.
Aliya	Read Gapology Book	Include in Planning Meetings
Javier	Spend a day with Michael	Leverage During Conference Calls
Sara	Partner with Emma	Increase Salary
Isaac	Partner with Michael	Provide Funding for Project
Li	Revisit Training Program	Increase Weekly Coaching
Matt	Create a Development Plan	Assign a Mentor
Lucia	Create a Development Plan	Assign a Mentor

NOW IT'S YOUR TURN

Talent	

Mindset	

Performance Predictor	

Name	Actions to Improve Talent	Actions to Improve Mindset

LEVELS OF DEPENDENCE

Figure 21, Dependence Ladder, helps leaders understand the behavior of team members that may be limiting their action and creating Action Gaps. Action will increase as a team member moves up the scale from dependence toward independence and finally to interdependence.

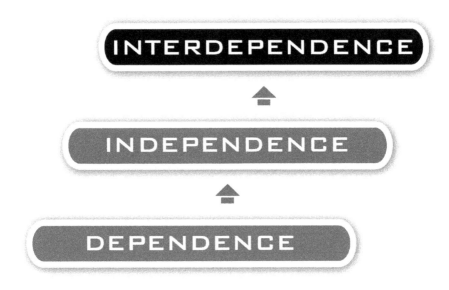

FIGURE 21 - DEPENDENCE LADDER

Here is a description of team member behavior fitting each level:

DEPENDENCE

Team members in this category need the support of others to fully execute their role. They drain the resources of the team. Some of the dependent team members are new in position, so being temporarily dependent is natural. As the leader, guide them from dependence to independence.

INDEPENDENCE

These team members are fully functioning and may even prefer operating on their own. They will likely perform well and meet expectations. The risk with independent team members is that they tend to operate in a silo and are more interested in their own performance than the team's success. Their behavior is consistent with cultures that are competitive, seeing the world in win/lose scenarios. If they are winning, the team performance is secondary. They will tend to be anti-team and anti-sharing. They take notes at your meetings but may not fully participate and contribute ideas back to the group. Counter this by involving them in team scenarios where winning is only achieved when everyone wins.

INTERDEPENDENCE

This is the highest level of team member behavior. Team members who work interdependently share their successes and work for the betterment of the entire team, not just themselves. They seek win/win solutions. Individual performance matters, but team performance is the primary focus. Anyone not performing stands out and is often forced out by the team. Working together, a team is much stronger than if the members are working independently and has fewer Action Gaps. Interdependent teams will self-manage gaps without the leader's involvement.

CULTURE OF ACTION

A culture of action is the desired outcome of Gapology and ultimately the difference between the winning leaders and the rest of the leaders we have studied.

We use the service industry model as an example, but you can apply it to your organization and industry. It will be helpful for you to define customers, team members, and leaders in your organization and apply those definitions to this model.

In a traditional service industry scenario, a culture of action occurs when the leader's behavior impacts the team member's behavior, creating action that, in turn, impacts the customer's behavior in a way that achieves the desired outcome of increased sales and profits. The customer's behavior then in turn impacts the leader's behavior, completing the cycle and starting the cycle once again. Most of this book up until this point has been about laying the groundwork for a culture of action.

For the purpose of Figure 22, the Culture of Action Model, we use the sales organization structure of XYZ:

FIGURE 22 - CULTURE OF ACTION MODEL

LEADER BEHAVIORS THAT INITIATE THE CULTURE OF ACTION

- Identify and Close the Knowledge Gaps.

- Identify and Close the Importance Gaps.

- Identify and Close the Action Gaps.

- Build a support structure to proactively identify and close gaps.

- Seek team member feedback about their mindset and their Performance Gaps.

- Seek customer feedback on performance compared to their expectations.

- Respond to team member and customer feedback, perpetuating the culture of action.

TEAM MEMBER ACTIONS THAT ARE THE OUTCOME OF LEADER BEHAVIOR AND CONTINUE THE CULTURE OF ACTION

- Know and Do the expected behavior, achieving the desired outcomes.

- Achieve Doing Level engagement while working toward Being Level engagement.

- Give leader feedback to impact mindset.

- Give leader feedback on Performance Gaps.

- Share customer feedback with the leader.

CUSTOMER ACTIONS THAT RESULT FROM TEAM MEMBER EXECUTION, THUS CONTINUING THE CULTURE OF ACTION

- Shift in spending patterns supporting desired behavior.

- Buying more and spending more.

- Increased frequency of purchasing.

- Create word of mouth about desired behaviors.

- Give feedback on experience.

The leader's behavior is the starting point for the culture of action. Winning leaders have learned how to create and sustain a culture of action. Our attempt to explain it is certainly oversimplified, and you will need to apply it to your own organization. Be prepared for a significant trial-and-error period prior to success.

MADDY'S STORY
BEING THE MESSAGE

Knowing, Doing, and Being represent the most powerful learning from my Gapology experience. My learnings in total were beyond life changing, as they allowed me to help hundreds, maybe thousands of others change their lives, too, but Knowing, Doing, and Being seem to bring it all together for me. As a leader, they allow me to clearly see my team and myself in the pure light of engagement.

One season, we were given a stretch target by XYZ, representing a 20 percent sales increase in a specific category of product. While that sounds aggressive, when Knowing, Doing, and Being were applied at all levels, it became easy. I will tell you the end of the story first. We hit a 31 percent sales increase!

Here was my simple plan:

> I assembled the sales manager team for a half-day meeting. When they arrived, I presented the 20 percent challenge. I then asked the following questions:
>> Why does beating 20 percent matter to our team?
>> What does Being Level behavior look like for a sales rep, sales manager, and a district manager?
>> How will we create Being Level behavior at all levels?

Our Actions:

> My team committed to the 20 percent goal very quickly. They felt that a major challenge like this would either impact negatively or solidify our top-shelf reputation, depending upon the outcome. We were all in on beating 20 percent!

> Next, we defined for the rep level, sales manager level, and district manager level what behaviors were needed to equal Being. Each sales manager would hold a quick half-day meeting this week with the reps to lie out the plan.

> We agreed to measure weekly and recap back to the team.

We made it look easy. Our 31 percent increase was not difficult for us, and yet it led the company!

The ability to define Being level for all levels was the key to success.

The other teams were stuck in the Doing mode, and Being beats Doing every time. Being is like Doing squared.

MADDY'S LESSONS

KDB, as I like to call it, is very powerful. First you look inside of yourself, then to your team. You must learn to "be the message" you are delivering to your team. That is one of my favorite sayings, but it is much more. As leader, you must embody the message of change.

GAPOLOGY LESSONS
CULTURE
ROOT SOLUTION

A culture of action is the desired model for every organization. Imagine a team so closely aligned with the vision of the organization that everyone acts without being told.

Gapology is a roadmap for changing an organization by changing behaviors. At the heart of this change is a change in mindset. Mindset is the launching pad for behavioral change.

One method of measuring the mindset level of team members and leaders is by identifying if they are at the Knowing, Doing, or Being Levels. When the leader is at a Being Level, the team shifts toward Being Level as well. They have no choice. This shifting of mindset becomes the true catalyst for behavioral change that will launch an organization into what we call a culture of action.

Leaders in key positions must achieve Being Level mindset for great success to take hold and become part of the company's culture. At the Being Level, Action Gaps are proactively closed and even prevented.

Winning leaders live at the Being Level in the most important things.

Here are some things you must consider to become a winning leader and create a winning organization:

- What programs or processes are critical to the success of your organization?
- Where does your engagement fall, Knowing, Doing, or Being Level, in relation to these programs?
- If you say Being, would your team agree? Do they see Being Level when they look at your behavior?

We use an equation to predict the performance of an individual or a team. It has proven quite effective and quite accurate.

The equation is $T \times M = P$.

T is for Talent, M is for Mindset or state of mind, and P is for Performance.

All leaders have a significant impact on Mindset. We can't forget that. Winning leaders work hard to have a positive impact on the mindset of their team.

One of the characteristics of the teams of winning leaders is their high level of empowerment and a subsequent high level of engagement. They do not wait for direction. They take action. This action leads to high levels of performance.

The Dependence Ladder helps leaders understand the behavior of team members that may be limiting their action and creating Action Gaps. Action will increase as a team member moves up the scale from dependence toward independence and finally to interdependence.

- Dependence
- Independence
- Interdependence

A culture of action is the desired outcome of Gapology and ultimately the difference between the winning leaders and the rest of the leaders we have studied.

Leader behaviors that initiate the culture of action:

- Identify and Close the Knowledge Gaps.
- Identify and Close the Importance Gaps.
- Identify and Close the Action Gaps.
- Build a support structure to proactively identify and close gaps.
- Seek team member feedback about their mindset and their Performance Gaps.
- Seek customer feedback on performance compared to their expectations.
- Respond to team member and customer feedback, perpetuating the culture of action.

Team member actions that are the outcome of leader behavior and continue the culture of action:

- Know and Do the expected behavior, achieving the desired outcomes.
- Work toward the Being Level.
- Give leader feedback to impact mindset.
- Give leader feedback on Performance Gaps.
- Share customer feedback with the leader.

Customer actions that result from team member execution, thus continuing the culture of action:

- Shift in spending patterns supporting desired behavior.
- Buying more and spending more.
- Increased frequency of purchasing.
- Create word of mouth about desired behaviors.
- Give feedback on experience.

The leader's behavior is the starting point for the culture of action Winning leaders have learned how to create and sustain a culture of action.

PART 4

NEXT
STEPS

16

TEACHING ORGANIZATION

Teaching organizations are learning organizations. They are also winning organizations.

Most organizations do not qualify as teaching organizations because they don't understand the value of leaders teaching. They may value learning, but that simply puts the ownership on the learner. It is much different to put the ownership on the leaders, as teachers. Most organizations are built on a foundation of hierarchy or chain of command. Leaders stay out of the weeds, and the trainers' job is to teach. They mistakenly believe that the leaders aren't teachers, and their role is to simply drive profit.

"When teaching becomes a value, the potential of an organization becomes boundless."

Although profit is the reason for most organizations, an organization built on the foundation of teaching as a value can become a superior profit-generating organization as well.

TEACHING ORGANIZATION PYRAMID

When teaching becomes a value, and teachers are developed at all levels, the potential and sustainability of the organization become boundless. Teaching, as a value, is the entry point for climbing the Teaching Organization Pyramid, as shown in Figure 23, to ultimately achieve organizational wisdom.

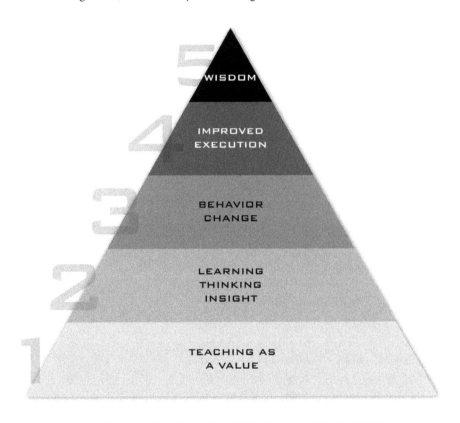

FIGURE 23 - TEACHING ORGANIZATION PYRAMID MODEL

Let's examine each of the levels of the Teaching Organization Pyramid:

LEVEL ONE: TEACHING AS A VALUE

LEVEL TWO: LEARNING/THINKING/INSIGHT

LEVEL THREE: BEHAVIOR CHANGE

LEVEL FOUR: IMPROVED EXECUTION

LEVEL FIVE: WISDOM

LEVEL ONE
TEACHING AS A VALUE

Teaching as a value is the entry point of the Teaching Organization Pyramid. True teaching organizations create a solid foundation for long-term growth. They create a replacement mentality, where internal promotion is a reality and a requirement. Leaders are responsible for preparing their replacements. They own the teaching and sharing of knowledge and skills, thus growing the competencies of their team. You may have heard of learning organizations, but learning is a one-way street. Teaching and creating leaders who teach is a four-lane superhighway by comparison.

Teaching organizations are capable of creating results that other companies admire from afar and can't comprehend. Teaching creates energy in both the teacher and in the learner that makes work exciting.

The success of winning leaders is built upon teaching as a competency, a passion, and a part of their daily rhythm. They develop "Teachable Points of View" or TPOVs, to pass on the teaching to their teams. Teaching is on purpose and intentional. It creates an environment of replacement leadership where internally grown leaders are ready for every open position.

Each leader should develop a series of TPOV teachings, ready for delivery to their teams, whether spontaneous or planned. These TPOVs allow leaders to easily step into the teaching mode at any time. As you may recall from the Knowledge Gap section of Gapology, they take on various forms; Stump Speech, Creating a Shared Vision, Making the Business Case, New Process Demonstration, and Selling Change.

These TPOVs can be taken by the learners and taught to others, thus creating more teachers. Teaching creates teaching. The ideal scenario is for your direct reports to take your TPOVs and, make them their own, putting them in their own words, with their style, and teaching their direct reports, peers, and others.

If a leader has ten team members, and they each have ten team members, one TPOV can teach one hundred team members. If you develop and instruct a new TPOV each period of the year for your total team, you will have spread twelve hundred teachings.

Wisdom can be achieved when you truly multiply your own efforts. Teaching as a value becomes contagious and creates a culture of teaching that can potentially lead to organizational wisdom.

LEVEL TWO
LEARNING/THINKING/INSIGHT

Teaching creates learning, and learning sharpens thinking.

An organization that has a culture of learning and thinking is likely an industry leader.

Learning and thinking are competitive advantages for organizations because learning and thinking create insight.

Insight is a powerful thing to possess. Insight forms the foundation for decision-making. For those who say they don't have the time for their leaders to be teachers, we suggest that you think again because you may be shortsighted.

Through a Gapology lens, learning and thinking organizations close Knowledge Gaps and Importance Gaps without continuous leader intervention and fire-fighting.

Closing gaps at the lowest level within an organization is always desired. Closing gaps is an exercise in empowerment, which has long-range impact for the empowered individual.

As the Gapology team travels across the country and meets with leadership teams, we are often asked questions about how to do something. Our answer is routinely thrown back in the form of a question, "What do you think?"

When given an answer, we will ask, "Why?" Our purpose is to create thinking and insight. We will give our opinion or share our experience, but then we come back to, "What do you think?" This always keeps us in the learning mode. Some of the best ideas come from remaining curious and gaining the thinking and insight of others.

Our suggested practice is to always make the business case around any expectation you have for your team, but let the team member paint the business case. Then you, as the leader, should just fill in the blanks or correct any misunderstanding.

Winning leaders are slow to give answers, but quick to listen to answers given. Leaders who just give answers will not create an empowered, gap-closing, results-driven team. They will create a team that waits and waits. They will wait to act until they get direction from the boss, and this creates Action Gaps.

So, you should rarely give the answer, but instead work to create insight. The learning is always in the thinking and figuring it out, not in what you are told.

LEVEL THREE
BEHAVIOR CHANGE

At this level, the learning, thinking, and insight manifest themselves in behavior change.

- Insight creates empowerment.

- Empowerment creates action.

In that action, you will find behavior change. So, at Level Three, Action Gaps are being closed and things are getting done.

Are they the right things? Most likely, if Levels One and Two have taught the right things and created the right learning. Strong leadership and recurring "teaching with a purpose" are critical here.

Let's take another example from Maddy's team.

Maddy created a Teachable Point of View (TPOV) around the three-step selling process. She uses this TPOV each time she meets with a sales manager and his or her sales rep team. She also meets with all new sales reps to personally deliver her TPOV, helping them close any and all gaps around the three-step process. In this TPOV, she makes the business case for the three-step process, tells of specific successes that sales reps have had using the process, and then models the process in an actual skills practice with the sales reps.

Toward the end of the teaching, she has the reps skill practice, two at a time, with customer rep scenarios she has created.

To conclude, she asks the reps to discuss what they have learned and what behavior change they will make immediately. She then turns to the sales manager and asks the same questions. Maddy states her expectations that the sales manager will repeat her teaching segment with his or her sales reps and make it their own.

She then asks each sales rep for his or her commitment to deliver the three-step process with each customer. She asks each individually, "Do you commit?" Each rep answers back, "I do!" Although redundant and forced, it closes the Importance Gap when verified and followed up on.

- Do you see how she has captured Levels One, Two, and Three with one powerful TPOV?
- Do you think she has impacted behavior change in sales managers and sales reps?
- Do you see the insight gained at both the manager and rep levels?
- Has she closed the Knowledge Gap with regard to the three-step selling process? Has she also closed the Importance Gap?

We say, "yes" to both of those gaps and would add that she has likely closed the Action Gap with many on her team by moving them toward Level Four—Improved Execution.

LEVEL FOUR
IMPROVED EXECUTION

Level Four is built on a solid foundation where the Knowledge and Importance Gaps have been closed. This foundation creates the platform for significantly improved execution, which will ultimately lead to great performance. The team is now armed and ready. The right action is automatic. Leaders who have laid this foundation have removed any excuses for poor performance. The team can't say, "We didn't know what was expected."

In Level Four, you can expand the teaching and make a move toward sustained great performance. The sharing of best methods and the development of new and better performance models become possible because base performance levels are in place. Improved execution allows you to focus on bigger, more important actions. You are not tied down with the basics because Performance Gaps are at a minimum. Teams begin to proactively anticipate gaps and build execution strategies to eliminate gaps before they occur. When there are gaps, team members and leaders recognize them, call them out, and close them. When results do not meet expectations, autopsies are conducted to find gaps that were missed so they can be closed immediately.

Team members who are not producing results come under significant scrutiny because they stand out, as do the behaviors that led to the poor results. Often, team members will force out peer underperformers without leadership involvement. Winning becomes cultural and no one is allowed to stand in the way. Underperformers do not feel comfortable in this culture and will likely find an environment with lower expectations.

LEVEL FIVE
WISDOM

Teaching organizations create a solid foundation for the long-term growth of an organization because they create institutional wisdom.

How does teaching ultimately create wisdom? This question is much easier to answer than it is to do. Wisdom does not automatically result from teaching, and most organizations have a wisdom gap.

Wisdom closes Knowledge Gaps, makes Importance Gaps disappear, and prevents Action Gaps. It also comes over time and must pass through the maze of an organization.

One interesting characteristic of winning leaders and organizations that have achieved Level Five-Wisdom, is how they get things done. They are very deliberate about how they move their teams to action.

It flows like this:

- They tell the team what they need to know.

- They tell the team why it matters.

- They tell the team what action they need to take.

Does this look familiar? It should, because it is the sequential flow of Gapology. Winning leaders and organizations close the Knowledge Gap, then the Importance Gap, and then the Action Gap. They do this every time action and movement of the team is needed. It works, and it is no different than how you might structure an ad campaign or a sales pitch. It seems to not be present in leaders and teams that have not achieved wisdom, but it becomes standard procedure for those that have.

Here is another characteristic of winning leaders and organizations that we discovered. They impart knowledge in order to create wisdom.

Here are the four steps that take the knowledge imparted during teaching and turn it into wisdom:

TESTED

Knowledge must be tested over time to become wisdom. You have heard of the phrase "tried-and-tested" when it comes to an idea or a process used by an organization. This is one of the filters that ideas are passed through on the way to becoming institutional wisdom.

MEASURED

The outcome of the imparted knowledge that is converted to action must be measured. The best idea in the world that does not produce the desired result is worthless.

TIMELESS

Knowledge takes time to become wisdom. Great organizations treat wisdom like a treasure that gets better over time. Leaders tell stories and impart institutional knowledge to others who become leaders and tell stories of their own. Along the way, these leaders use the knowledge learned from the stories and create successes that lead to more stories.

TEACHABLE

Knowledge that becomes wisdom can be shared and passed on from one organizational generation to the next. Leaders teach with a purpose. It becomes an art form. Teaching is how big things get done.

MADDY'S STORY
WISDOM

Gapology changed XYZ in more ways than I can describe. I am proud to have been a part of the success and fortunate to be there to see it. It changed XYZ because it changed its leaders and eventually the entire team. We moved from third in the industry to a dominant #1, selling the same products and services as the rest.

How? Let me try to explain. I don't think I have the complete answer, but I was there and I was part of it, so my view is pretty clear.

First off, Gapology and the process of identifying and closing gaps made us much more productive. We executed much better. That was big, and it impacted all levels of the company very quickly. It was easy to grasp and leverage.

Secondly, Gapology allowed us to look forward and close gaps that hadn't occurred yet. This made us bulletproof. We could literally out-execute everyone in every way. This is where the wisdom started kicking in. We could predict what would go wrong before it went wrong and put actions in place to prevent it. This made execution of programs and events a game. Tools like the Habit Ladder helped us here. We anticipated gaps in team execution and overcame them with training and practice.

Lastly, and most importantly, we became better leaders. Once we got a taste of Being, we knew what leadership and greatness were all about. It shaped us by shaping our view of our role. We reached Being in the things that mattered. We hired Being Level leaders. This is where our wisdom solidified because we created wisdom in levels below us, so as succession occurred, we didn't miss a beat. The Commitment Ladder was a tool we leveraged to gain insight into our team, and once again we got wiser.

At the end of the day, organizational wisdom became our reality. The team stuck around, too. Everyone knew they were part of something special, and they wanted to see it through. Gapology has been the greatest experience in my lifetime. Open up to the possibilities.

GAPOLOGY LESSONS
TEACHING ORGANIZATION

Teaching organizations are learning organizations. They are also winning organizations.

The Teaching Organization Pyramid Model represents the power of developing a teaching organization and the ultimate goal of achieving organizational wisdom.

Most organizations do not qualify as teaching organizations because they don't understand the value of leaders teaching. They may value learning, but that simply puts the ownership on the learner. It is much different to put the ownership on the leaders as teachers. Most organizations are built on a foundation of hierarchy or chain of command. Leaders stay out of the weeds, and the trainers' job is to teach. They mistakenly believe that the leaders aren't teachers, and their role is to simply drive profit.

When teaching becomes a value, and teachers are developed at all levels, the potential and sustainability of the organization become boundless.

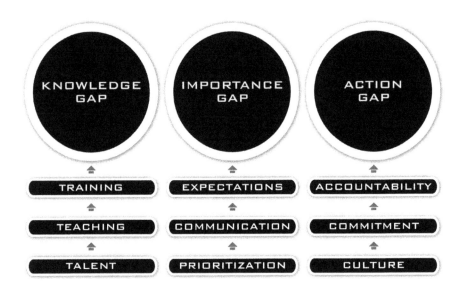

17

GETTING STARTED

So, now you understand the three types of Performance Gaps and the Root Solutions to close them.

You have explored the leader behaviors to identify and close each gap, and you have tested the Root Solutions for closing each gap. You have read how Maddy applied each Root Solution to close gaps in her team.

You are well on your way to becoming a real Gapologist, so now what?

"Remember, Performance Gaps get closed in sequential order; Knowledge, Importance, then Action."

GAP MAPPING

Review the sample Gap Mapping table below including the Root Solutions. This tool represents the easiest way to start.

WHAT & HOW	WHY & WHEN	THE CHOICE
TRAINING	EXPECTATIONS	ACCOUNTABILITY
TEACHING	COMMUNICATION	COMMITMENT
TALENT	PRIORITIZATION	CULTURE

What recurring Performance Gap has been identified?	Is it a Knowledge, Importance, or Action Gap or a combination?
(Step 1 Here)	(Step 2 Here)

BEHAVIORS vs. EXPECTATIONS	ROOT SOLUTION APPLIED	ACTIONS/TIMING/ OWNERS
What behavior was exhibited vs. expected behavior?	Describe the determined Root Solution to close the gap:	Describe the specific actions to undertake and any time frames along with the owners of actions:
(Step 3 Here)	(Step 4 Here)	(Step 5 Here)

Here are the steps to take:

STEP 1

Define the most significant Performance Gaps you are experiencing. These gaps should be defined in both behavior and result terms. Involve the leaders who are responsible for closing the gaps. You may want to involve key team members as well.

As you discuss the gaps, limit yourself to the top two or three. Rank them in priority order and start with the top-ranked gap. List it in its simplest form. Maddy's team, for example, might define the identified gap as "Missing Sales Plan."

STEP 2

Determine for the gap identified if it is a Knowledge, Importance, or Action Gap, or some combination of the three. Many Performance Gaps will have elements of each.

As you will recall:

- Knowledge Gaps are gaps in "what" to do and "how" to do it.
- Importance Gaps are gaps in "why" it matters and "when" it must be done.
- Action Gaps are a choice, once the Knowledge and Importance Gaps are closed.

All Performance Gaps are gaps in behavior and expectations. Using Maddy's team as an example, she found Knowledge, Importance, and Action Gaps in the execution of the three-step selling process (behavior) causing the team to miss the sales plan (expectations).

Remember, Performance Gaps should be closed in sequential order: Knowledge, Importance, then Action.

STEP 3

Determine for the gap identified the specific behaviors and the expectations miss. This will help you identify the appropriate Root Solution and begin focusing your efforts on the proper leadership methods needed for your action plan. Using Maddy's team as an example, she found the three-step selling process was not implemented resulting in the miss to sales plan.

STEP 4

Determine each Root Solution required to close the gap.

STEP 5

Assign specific actions to apply the Root Solution in order to close the gap. Be very intentional about areas of responsibility and ensure that the owners of the action steps are the right people. Leverage the power of the larger team when possible, creating a shared vision around closing the gap. Be sure to apply timeframes and follow-up dates to create accountability.

Share the action steps with all stakeholders, gaining their support and commitment. Ask what support may be needed, and be prepared to play an active role as leader.

Congratulations! You are on your way to closing the gap.

Repeat this process for each type of identified Performance Gap: Knowledge, Importance and Action.

FINAL WORDS

GAPOLOGY IS A JOURNEY

Finishing the reading of *Gapology* is just the first step in your journey. Your skills in identifying and closing Performance Gaps will grow each time you step up to improve results. As you develop further, however, you may

> *"A journey of a thousand miles must begin with a single step."*
>
> -Chinese Proverb

begin seeing more gaps than before. This doesn't mean they weren't there before. You just couldn't see them.

As you see and tackle more gaps, your performance will accelerate. You will begin using your Gapology skills in advance and take proactive measures to improve performance. Identifying Performance Gaps in you and in the team can be a very humbling experience, but one that will move you forward on your journey in life.

Soon, after consistent practice you will find that your skills as a Gapologist have achieved the Habit Level. By then you will have already tasted the sweetness of being a winning leader, and you will know that you are traveling down a path known only by a select few.

While you enjoy the ride, take time to pass the word by teaching Gapology to others. The greatest success in life comes when you help others achieve their dreams.

EXECUTIVE SUMMARY

The purpose of the Executive Summary is twofold:

- Allow Gapologists, those that have read the book, to have a quick summary of each chapter for a quick refresher. True Gapologists teach Gapology to their teams in order to create a Teaching Organization, so bringing the Executive Summary together at the end of the book is simply a convenience.

- Allow future Gapologists, those that have not read the book yet, to gain a quick overview of the book and to gain general knowledge of all Gapology concepts within an hour. So, in this case, the Executive Summary is more of a service. It is truly the "CliffsNotes" of Gapology.

The Executive Summary flows in chapter order and is the aggregate of the Gapology Lessons at the end of each chapter.

INTRODUCTION

Gaps happen.

They happen in every company, department, work team, and individual performer every day.

Gaps account for trillions of dollars of lost revenue and profit each year.

Performance Gaps are the number-one risk to all companies and organizations today. By contrast, leaders and teams that have the fewest gaps and close those gaps quickest win. They win by big margins.

Winning leaders spend a significant amount of time observing their team's behavior, comparing that behavior to the expectation. They then compare the actual results produced to the result expectations. This directly connects the behaviors to the results and highlights any Performance Gaps. The better the behavior, the better the results. Gaps in behavior create gaps in results.

Gapology is the term we developed to describe what winning leaders do to identify and close Performance Gaps in their teams. Gapology is their process.

The sample group for Gapology was limited to the top 10 percent in performance, the A-Group, and the bottom 10 percent in performance, the C-Group. We also refer to the A-Group as the "winning leaders" and the C-Group as the "not winning leaders." We wanted to understand the difference between these true outlying performance groups. The middle 80 percent, the B-Group, was not the focus of our study.

To determine their performance we looked only at the leader's five most directly controllable and comparable metrics:

- Sales to budget (P&L)
- Profit to budget (P&L)
- Customer satisfaction (ongoing survey scores)
- Team satisfaction (annual survey)
- Team turnover (annual rate)

These metrics also aligned with their annual performance measures, thus providing a level playing field and best way to define "winning" for the leaders measured.

As you might expect, the gap in results between the A-Group and the C-Group in our study was very large! Unfortunately, the performance of the winning leaders was literally being canceled out by the poor performance of those not winning; The C-Group canceled out the positive performance of the A-Group. Because of this, the performance of the total team was limited to the performance of the middle, the B-Group.

The reason for the gap became more clearly defined when the leadership behaviors and tactics of the A and C-Groups are observed. The A-Group shared a common thread. They moved to action by identifying and closing Performance Gaps in themselves and in their teams. Without knowing it and without a common playbook, the A-Group followed a similar sequential path to winning that is not present in the C-Group.

Winning leaders close Performance Gaps by taking action and moving their teams to take action. Taking the right action is key to closing Performance Gaps.

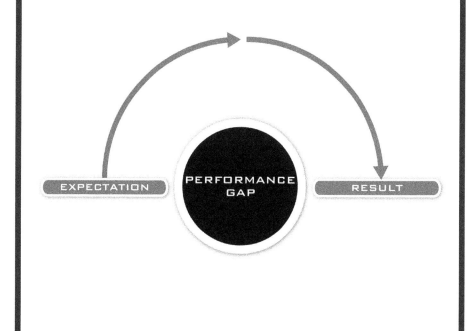

In the Performance Gap Model, you will see that Performance Gaps are the gaps between what you expect and the actual outcome. Performance Gaps are gaps in behavior that also create gaps in results.

All Performance Gaps are Knowledge, Importance, Action, or some combination of the three! There are no other types of Performance Gaps.

KNOWLEDGE GAPS
THE "WHAT" AND THE "HOW"

> Winning leaders ensure that their teams know "what" actions to take and then "how" to take them. This closes Knowledge gaps.

IMPORTANCE GAPS
THE "WHY" AND THE "WHEN"

> Winning leaders ensure that their teams know "why" an action is important and "when" it must be done. This closes Importance Gaps.

ACTION GAPS
THE "CHOICE"

> Action Gaps mean that despite knowing "what" to do and "how" to do it, as well as knowing "why" it is critical and "when" it must be done, the right action is not taken. Action Gaps are therefore a choice.

Gapology can be taught and will spread throughout your organization, as well as become a source of great personal development for those who learn to apply it. Once your eyes and your mind are open to Gapology, your performance as a leader will be changed forever. You will see things you didn't see before. It will influence what you hear when having conversations with your team. It will shape your actions following the analysis of results. You will begin seeing gaps everywhere, even outside of your professional life.

As a leader, you will often find that you are the gap, or at least the source of the gap. Your behavior may actually be hindering the performance of your team. Be prepared and open to looking in the mirror. Gapology and identifying and closing Performance Gaps can appear deceptively simple so don't be fooled. Winning leaders make winning look easy, but that is often the outcome of significant learning through trial and error. Winning leaders learn from their failures. They don't fear failure, and they don't get frustrated and give up. They simply identify and close Performance Gaps, and each time they learn and grow from the process.

Winning leaders showed us that the sequence matters. You can't close Action Gaps without the Knowledge and Importance Gaps being closed. It won't work.

Consider the following a sequential example of closing Performance Gaps in your team:

- "My team knows what to do and how to do it." Knowledge Gaps closed.
- "My team knows why it must be done and when it must be done." Importance Gaps closed.
- "My team makes the choice to take action and achieves the expected outcome." Action Gaps closed.

Review the Gapology Model. This represents the full Gapology process, including the Root Solutions, that winning leaders use to identify and close Performance Gaps. Memorize this model.

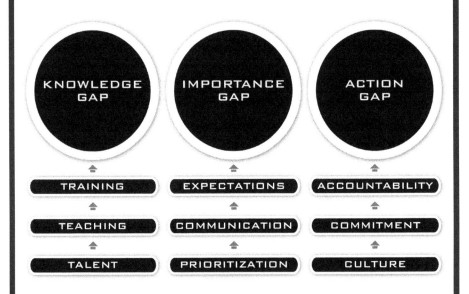

KNOWLEDGE GAPS

Knowledge Gaps are the gaps between what we don't know and what we do know.

Knowledge Gaps are the result of either a lack of knowledge or a lack of skill. Many leaders focus only on providing knowledge and ignore developing and validating skills. Winning leaders do not make this mistake.

Closing Knowledge Gaps is the first step in great performance. Most often, the lowest-level team member is directly interfacing with the customer and is therefore responsible for taking the correct action. Knowledge Gaps can be devastating to performance here. Closing Knowledge Gaps can often be as simple as having the team member demonstrate and practice the desired behavior. During this time, the leader's behavior should be to encourage, coach, and recognize the team member's actions until the desired behavior becomes habit. Combine this with setting clear expectations that the behavior is to be repeated, and you are well on your way to closing the Knowledge Gaps.

Some leaders make the mistake of assuming that their team knows a behavior because they have been trained. They compound the mistake by thinking a behavior will be sustained. Most training fails to close all Knowledge Gaps.

The Knowledge Gaps of the leader cause Knowledge Gaps in the team and they often go unidentified, undiscussed, and therefore unclosed. Winning leaders show a high level of self-awareness of their own gaps.

Performance Gaps manifest themselves in behavior and results, or both. The results show the gaps in behavior, and the gaps in behavior predict the gaps in results.

Curiosity is a key quality of winning leaders, and it is a key to identifying gaps. We have found that winning leaders are always asking why some results are good and other results are bad. The answers to these simple questions lead them directly to gaps in performance because the questions and subsequent answers expose the gaps.

Gaps must first be identified if they are to be closed.

You can't close a gap you don't see!

If you don't ask questions, you become the gap!

We discovered six winning leader behaviors to identify Knowledge Gaps.

Winning Leader Behaviors to Identify Knowledge Gaps:

- *Review actual results versus expectations.*
- *Observe behavior versus expectations.*
- *Ask questions about results and behavior. Be curious.*
- *Listen to the answers completely before follow-up.*
- *Avoid blaming. Keep focused on identifying the gap.*
- *Ask confirming questions to determine the gap.*

Identifying Knowledge Gaps is the first step winning leaders use to drive great performance. Follow these six steps and you will identify the true Performance Gaps.

Closing Knowledge Gaps looks simple.

Winning leaders verify Knowledge Gaps are closed, and when gaps do occur, they look for their personal gaps first. Knowledge Gaps most often originate with the leader, so it is up to the leader to close them.

Winning leaders know that their personal behavior matters, and when a team is not performing, they look at their own behavior first. The gaps in the leader's behavior should be the highest priority because they create gaps in the team.

When your team is not performing to your expectations, start by looking in the mirror. What are your Performance Gaps?

Closing Knowledge Gaps alone does not equal winning. A winning performance is achieved when the all gaps are closed.

There are six winning leader behaviors utilized to close Knowledge Gaps.

Winning Leader Behaviors to Close Knowledge Gaps:

- *Declare the Knowledge Gaps.*
- *Seek feedback on the declaration.*
- *Ask for solutions and accept blame.*
- *Gain commitment to the solutions offered.*
- *Set expectations.*
- *Follow up and verify the commitment.*

ROOT SOLUTION: TRAINING

The first step to take when a Knowledge Gap is identified is to determine if there may be a training issue.

Many leaders overestimate the effectiveness and retention of training. Training often leaves Knowledge Gaps because many times training is delivered in a one-dimensional format, just focusing on providing knowledge and not on building skills and commitment to the point where the performance becomes a habit. Team members are just talked to or told to read something. The trainer creates the gap by assuming that they have the skills and commitment to consistently perform to the expected level.

Remember this quote: "Telling ain't training!"

We recommend the use of a simple ladder to gauge the point of retention of a trainee during the training process. The following flow works for most training situations and is what we call the Habit Ladder. Moving training to the Habit Level should be the objective of the training of a task or process.

The Habit Ladder is one of our favorite tools to measure the effectiveness of training and the likely performance levels of teams. Here is the Ladder and descriptions from Maddy's team and the execution of the new three-step selling process:

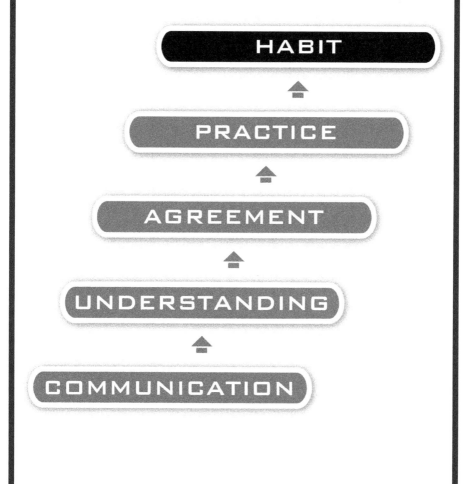

COMMUNICATION

My sales manager has told me about the three-step process.

UNDERSTANDING

I have had my questions answered, and I understand the three-step process in theory.

AGREEMENT

I agree to use the three-step process with all of my customers, and I understand what is expected of me. I am committed to the process.

PRACTICE

I have role-played the three-step process with my sales manager and peers and have shown the ability to effectively execute all three steps with customers.

HABIT

I use the three-step process with every customer and have experienced the success that comes from the three steps. I am an expert, committed to the process, and an advocate to my peers.

One of the most misunderstood and least considered factors in training is that people learn differently, specifically adults. If the design of your training is "one size fits all," you are likely creating Performance Gaps.

If you assume that the Knowledge Gap is a result of a training issue, retrain. But where a process or task is involved, be sure to retrain to the Habit Level. Only then will you close that gap. If the gap recurs, you will know the root cause is something else.

Recurring Knowledge Gaps by the same team member suggest that you have the wrong person in the role. Retraining can be a trap that hides the real issue.

The Four Key Rules of Adult Learning:

- Adults learn when they feel the need to learn and the content is relevant to them personally.
- Adults learn best when their unique experiences are considered.
- Adults learn best and retain more when a variety of instructional approaches and contexts are used.
- Adults need practice and feedback until successful in a behavior.

Here are some of the tactics we learned from winning leaders that you can also use to leverage the four key rules in your meetings and training:

- Give adults the business case for the learning. Tell them why it is critical and what it will do for them. Make the learning nonnegotiable and set expectations. Lead off with this tactic.
- Ask them to design or have input on their own training agenda and have them develop a list of topics they feel they will need more or less of. Get their input into the agenda of a meeting or conference call
- Design meetings with a variety of delivery media: group discussion; visual, individual, and group work sessions; and pre-work and post-meeting assignments. Measure the outcomes of training and meetings with testing and feedback surveys.
- Create hands-on training where possible and provide feedback. Assign mentors for ongoing feedback and follow-up.

Great performance means minimizing the Knowledge Gaps not only with your team, but with your customers, too. Winning companies have figured this out and can be a source of learning for all leaders.

ROOT SOLUTION: TEACHING

One of the keys to closing ongoing Knowledge Gaps is for leaders to perform a teaching role.

In our research, leaders in the C-Group exclusively overlook this strategy. They tend to "tell" or "command" but not teach. We consider this a common thread in their poor performance.

Winning leaders know that teaching is key to achieving organizational wisdom. They develop and deliver "Teachable Points of View," or TPOVs for short, to their teams, remaining in the teaching mode at all times. They carve teaching into their daily rhythm, using teaching in short bursts to create learning and close Knowledge Gaps in their teams.

TPOVs take on various forms:

- Stump Speech
- Creating a Shared Vision
- Making the Business Case
- New Process Demonstration
- Selling Change

During times of change, leadership is the lighthouse in the fog of uncertainty. Winning leaders navigate the treacherous waters just fine, while the rest clearly struggle. Leaders need to devote extra time each day to "sell" the change.

Use these questions to structure your notes:

- Why the change? Make the business case.
- Why do you personally embrace the change?
- How will it impact the team member? Address their number-one concern.
- What does the team member need to do now? Create a sense of urgency and a call to action.

Winning leaders excel in leading through change. This is a strength and core competency, and it really separates winning from losing and is a powerful predictor of success.

When leading through change and confronting direct reluctance to change, refer to the DABA Change Ladder.

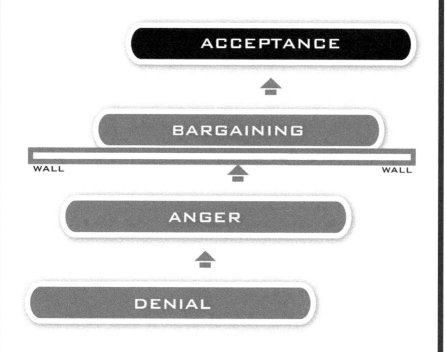

Watch for these specific phases in yourself and your team. You will discover that the anger phase is actually a good sign because it suggests that there is movement away from the denial phase.

During any major change, winning leaders over communicate to achieve acceptance and buy-in from their team. Use the DABA Change Ladder and observe the behavior of key team members during change to be most effective.

ROOT SOLUTION: TALENT

Ultimately, the more talented and skilled the team you lead, the fewer Knowledge Gaps you will experience.

Talent matters, and putting the right person in the right role makes a huge difference in performance.

Winning leaders spend a significant amount of time hiring and developing talent. It is often their primary focus because it creates their competitive edge. They know that for closing Performance Gaps, talent with the right mindset trumps everything else. In fact, when it comes to performance, winning leaders know that talent is a key ingredient, whether they've developed the talent organically or acquired it externally.

When winning leaders make changes to the team and move people from one position or location to another, they do so very strategically.

Winning leaders' behavior when it comes to "people moves" is strategic and deliberate, thus, "Play chess, not checkers."

"Play chess" means that each people move is strategic, is thought-out, and has a purpose. It also means that leaders are planning future moves as they make each move.

We recommend a multidimensional team ranking process based upon three criteria: achievement of results, alignment with organizational values, and overall leadership qualities. We call this the Leadership Ranking. We also use a different multidimensional approach based upon three other criteria: sales volume, sales upside potential, and market complexity. We call this the Position Ranking. This ranking is effective for most sales organizations. You can modify the team ranking process using three different criteria to fit your organization's structure.

Winning leaders know that the ideal team produces great results, is aligned with the organization's values, and has strong leadership, thus creating a bright future for the organization.

With this process completed and with the Leadership and the Position Rankings in alignment, winning leaders separate themselves from the rest more than any other single tactic of which we are aware. This means the right person is in the right role.

Winning leaders share a philosophy of replacement leadership. They are always developing their replacement. They view it as their duty to the organization, but also as a way to strengthen and challenge the team in new directions.

Where do most leaders spend the bulk of their time? Yes, with the C-Players. This leaves the A-Players feeling undervalued and likely leaves them underdeveloped. Too often leaders believe that the A-Players need less attention and have less room to grow. Winning leaders suggest that this is totally false and that A-Players have the most room to grow. Winning leaders spend more personalized time with A-Players than any other group, followed by C-Players, then B-Players.

Winning leaders manage people unequally. They believe that leadership is not "one size fits all," and that it is more complex because what works to lead each team member may be different.

Winning leaders take the time to find out what works for each individual while finding their hot buttons and pushing them.

Other leaders may make the mistake of developing a style and expecting everyone to adapt to it. Winning leaders adapt to the circumstances and the players to maximize the performance of each team member. People are unique, and to lead them you must manage them unequally.

IMPORTANCE GAPS

Importance Gaps are the gaps between knowing an action and knowing its importance.

This is an area where the clarity of leaders is tested. With all that is asked of team members and leaders and all of the conflicting priorities and messages, things can fall through the cracks. Those things, of course, are Performance Gaps. Leaders need to make sure that the things that do inevitably fall through the cracks are never the big things.

Importance Gaps are often packaged as excuses like these:

- "We just didn't get to it. We ran out of time."
- "You gave me so much other stuff to do."
- "There are only twenty-four hours in a day! I will do it tomorrow."
- "I thought it was optional!"
- "I covered it at the meeting, but for some reason my team did not execute."

Winning Leader Behaviors to Identify Importance Gaps:

- *Review results versus expectations.*
- *Observe behavior versus expectations.*
- *Ask about key expectations.*
- *Listen for understanding and commitment to the expectations.*
- *Avoid blame. Their answers may reflect your leadership.*
- *Avoid blame. Their answers may reflect your leadership.*
- *Restate expectations and ask for commitment.*

Closing Importance Gaps is a leader's role.

Winning leaders are strong and clear about what matters. They make sure there is no room for doubt. In the absence of a leader's clarity about what is important, chaos fills the gap, and that chaos leads to gaps in productivity and performance.

Winning Leader Behaviors to Close Importance Gaps:

- *Review results versus expectations.*
- *Observe team behavior versus expectations.*
- *Declare the Importance Gaps.*
- *Accept blame and reset expectations.*
- *Ask for commitment and agree to the consequences for inaction.*
- *Follow up and verify commitments.*

ROOT SOLUTION: EXPECTATIONS

Let's start by dispelling the myth that expectations are simply goals. They aren't. Many leaders make the mistake of setting goals but not expectations.

Winning leaders know to do both. They are different. Goals are things to strive for. They are nice to have. They are targets and may be long range. Expectations are the things that the leader "expects" to be delivered and are nonnegotiable. They are "must-haves," and winning leaders create accountability around expectations.

A goal is much different. You may create a goal of beating the sales budget by 10 percent, so 110 percent of the sales budget is the goal. This would be nice to have, but is not the same as the nonnegotiable expectation. Everyone on the team should work to achieve the goal, but it is much different than the expectation.

Winning leaders require expectations to have both a behavioral and a result component.

As shown in Expectations Model, the expected result must be determined by verifying which behaviors will produce it and vice versa.

The expected behaviors must produce the expected result. They must work together. They are symbiotic and cannot stand-alone. Oftentimes leaders will set one or the other, but not both. They will provide the expected result but not the expected behavior that will actually produce that result. Or they will just focus on the behaviors but remain unclear about what expected result they want to see.

The power in setting clear expectations is achieved by winning leaders through the transfer of ownership. Once the team members know their expectations and have committed to them, the leader has successfully transferred ownership of those expectations.

We have found that many leaders miss the Importance Gaps that exist with their own boss. They are not clear on what their boss expects. Winning leaders own this, even if the boss doesn't. Some bosses just aren't good at sharing clear expectations, so they create gaps with their leaders. Winning leaders don't let this stand in their way. They find out what the boss's expectations are, period! No gaps!

Most leaders set goals but not expectations. Most expectations can actually be executed 100 percent of the time, if that becomes the leader's expectation and that expectation is passed on to the team.

ROOT SOLUTION: COMMUNICATION

Importance Gaps are most often the result of the leader's lack of clear communication.

Just like recurring Knowledge Gaps imply a talent issue with a team member, recurring Importance Gaps imply a clarity and prioritization issue with the leader.

Winning leaders assume nothing! They over communicate a clear message and ensure it is understood. Winning leaders use communication as a tool to win and do not take it for granted. They carefully select the correct type of communication that will be most effective in delivering the desired result. They leverage communication as a differentiator. It closes gaps. That is Gapology!

Clear, concise, and verified communication closes Importance Gaps. Winning leaders are very deliberate about communication. They are not random with communication because they know it impacts their team's behavior.

Winning leaders only conduct meetings with a purpose and an objective, designed to create action in the team. They do not meet to just to meet.

Here are tactics that winning leaders use to turn meetings into action:

- Agenda
- Objective
- Random Recaps
- Calls to Action
- Post-meeting Assignments

Performance Gaps exist because of the lack of clear leadership. Winning leaders create winning followers.

We found certain "guideposts" winning leaders use to create a culture of followership:

- Mission Statement
- Organizational Values
- Leadership Competencies

The following eight competencies best capture those possessed by winning leaders and represent a strong force in closing Performance Gaps:

Gapology Top Eight Winning Leader Competencies:

- Embracing Change
- Managerial Courage
- Communicator
- Results-Driven
- Motivator
- Active Listener
- Responsible
- Competitive

Simplicity in structure improves communication. Performance is enhanced in a simple structure. Action becomes automatic because the action is up to you. It can't be passed off as someone else's job. Communication also flows from the top to the bottom and the bottom to the top without interpretation or interruption. Extra layers can add support and expertise, but they can also create confusion, mixed messages, and productivity issues.

You must structure your meetings to set action as an objective and not just a hopeful outcome.

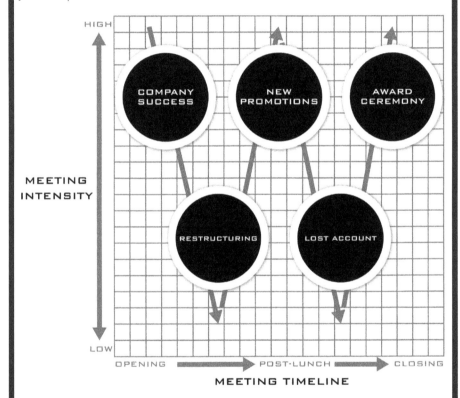

The Intensity W - Meeting Structure works for full or half-day meetings and structured conference calls or webinars. It works for any event where engagement of the audience matters. The concept is simple. View the W as an intensity meter vertically and a timeline horizontally.

There are three vertical high-intensity points: the beginning, the middle, and the end. There are two low points: one between the beginning and middle and the other between the middle and the end.

People remember two parts of a meeting more than any others: the opening and the closing.

Standing ovations are too rare, and they can really change people.

ROOT SOLUTION: PRIORITIZATION

Whoever first said, "If everything is important, nothing is important," knew about Importance Gaps. One of keys to closing Importance Gaps is always keeping the team focused on the priorities, especially when they are shifting.

Prioritization is about decision-making. When you know what matters because the priorities are clear, decisions are easier to make.

Leader behavior and actions must reflect the priorities. It really doesn't matter what the leader says or writes down. What matters most is what the leader does. Take, for instance, the leader who says that customer service is the number-one priority for their team and then ignores poor service or doesn't recognize good service, or even worse, does not personally model good customer service behavior when given the opportunity. This sends a confusing message to the team. The leader's behavior communicates the priorities to the team, whether intentional or not.

Clarity of priorities closes any potential Importance Gaps by creating a strong and compelling shared vision.

Creating a shared vision is significant because it creates a roadmap for closing Performance Gaps, specifically Importance and Action Gaps. For these gaps there is truly no greater way to align priorities than by creating a shared vision within your team.

Here are the steps in creating a shared vision that we learned from winning leaders:

- Start with the "Why."
- Make an Individual's Role Important.
- Keep the Vision Narrow, but Big.

ACTION GAPS

Action Gaps are the gaps between knowing the importance of an action and actually taking that action.

This is where the rubber meets the road in Gapology because it is all about the choice of the individual. Ultimately, he or she needs to make the choice to take action. This choice can be made consciously or subconsciously, but it is still a choice that is made or not made.

It may be the easiest gap to identify because it is the gap that is most obvious, but the Root Solutions are the most difficult.

Winning Leader Behaviors to Identify Action Gaps:

- *Review results and identify potential Performance Gaps.*
- *Observe team behavior where result expectations are not being met while looking for gaps.*
- *Inquire about key behavioral and result expectations and confirm understanding.*
- *Declare the gaps.*
- *Reset expectations and reiterate the consequences.*
- *Follow up for immediate behavior and result changes.*

Simply taking an action does not mean that it is the right action. There is a big difference between action and performance. When you get your team to take the right action, that action equals performance, and performance achieves the desired results. The "not winning" leaders, the C-Group, tend to react and blame when the team misses expectations. This causes their teams to spin and often take the wrong action.

Don't confuse being busy with being productive. Busy is action, but true productivity is performance (right action) that delivers desired results. Many people have simply learned to look productive.

Teams and organizations that do not keep score effectively may confuse the hard workers with the productive team members. In these organizations, there is no bridge from action to results.

Performance Gaps between performing to the expectations and not performing to the expectations can be subtle and hidden from a casual glance.

Action Gaps are the most difficult to close because the final ownership of taking action is now in the hands of the team. You have closed the Knowledge Gaps and the Importance Gaps, and your team is set to effectively close the Action Gaps.

Winning Leader Behaviors to Close Action Gaps:

- *Declare the Action Gaps.*
- *Inquire about expectations.*
- *Repeat expectations.*
- *Create accountability.*
- *Manage the gaps in performance.*
- *Apply recognition and consequences.*

Winning leaders never give up! They stay focused on closing gaps! Closing the gaps in sequential order (Knowledge, Importance, and then Action) creates the foundation for great performance and results.

ROOT SOLUTION: ACCOUNTABILITY

Winning leaders create accountability. They use a variety of different ways to do this, but the old-fashioned ways still works best.

- Set Expectations.
- Follow Up.
- Keep Score.
- Transfer Ownership.

Winning leaders use EDGE to create action and accountability.

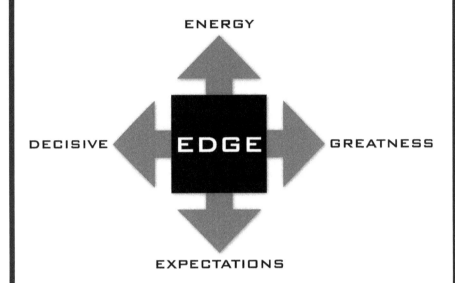

ENERGY

DECISIVE **EDGE** GREATNESS

EXPECTATIONS

As displayed above, the acronym of EDGE lays out the key elements that they consistently apply in their drive to win. EDGE is: Energy, Decisive, Greatness, and Expectations.

EDGE can be described as a strong point of view or belief in something. It is being unwavering and showing unwillingness to compromise on values and standards. It is not mean spirited. It brings others along because it is inspirational. EDGE is found in the winning leader's passion about that belief. It can be heard in how they speak. We developed the acronym to best fit the elements winning leaders bring to the game. They display and create Energy. They are Decisive. Greatness is their standard. Expectations are a tool they use to drive performance. So, EDGE fits winning leaders.

Progress is good, but it may inhibit achieving the expectations. Hold your team accountable for achieving the expectations versus over celebrating their progress.

A winning leader taught us the analogy that progress is like driving a car down a long highway and looking in the rearview mirror to see how far you have come. Expectations, where you are going, are not visible in the rearview mirror.

Winning leaders keep score. This became very clear to us during the interviews we conducted with leaders. Winning leaders, without exception, were connected to the key metrics of performance. They communicated the performance metrics to their team daily, weekly, each period, and often throughout the day. Winning leaders break down the metrics by team member to make the metrics real and meaningful. They also tie metrics to behavior. The C-Group by contrast was much less connected to metrics. Their teams were less aware of key metrics, and often, they were totally unaware of how the team was performing or how they were performing personally. One of the scariest characteristics we found in the C-Group teams was the view that their performance was "good," when the metrics suggested otherwise.

ROOT SOLUTION: COMMITMENT

One extremely powerful tool that you can use to contrast commitment and compliance levels on your team is the Commitment Ladder.

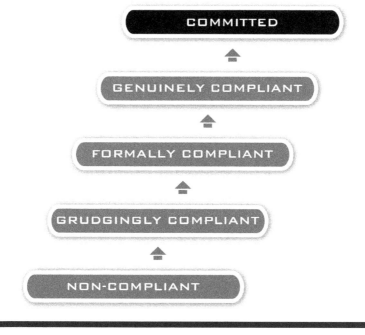

Leaders and team members who are committed or genuinely compliant to the vision of an organization will have fewer Action Gaps and will likely prevent them before they happen.

Charting your team's level of commitment is important and, as mentioned, should be applied independently to any significant initiative. Once charted, use the information to directly impact your leader behaviors. Winning leaders know that committed team members need to be treated differently than compliant team members. Each level has its own unique nuances and requires varied levels of direction and support, as does each individual person on the team.

If the direction and support is not appropriately applied, committed team members can slide down the Commitment Ladder, landing somewhere around the Grudgingly Compliant Level. We have found it helpful for leaders to measure the team's level of commitment or compliance toward the overall mission and expectations of the organization.

There are many things that generate commitment within an individual. Managing unequally is key. Commitment comes from within, but the leader can help light the fire. Using the Root Solutions from this book will also help to do that most effectively. Train, teach, and fill your team with talent. Set clear expectations using strong communication around the highest priorities. Establish methods of accountability and stay committed yourself to the people on your team and the company's mission, goals, and expectations. Finally, create a culture of action for your team. These Root Solutions can fix almost any commitment issue you encounter as a leader when the Performance Gaps are identified quickly and accurately.

ROOT SOLUTION: CULTURE

A culture of action is the desired model for every organization. Imagine a team so closely aligned with the vision of the organization that everyone acts without being told.

Gapology is a roadmap for changing an organization by changing behavior. At the heart of this change is a change in mindset. Mindset is the launching pad for behavioral change.

One method of measuring the mindset level of team members and leaders is by identifying if they are at the Knowing, Doing, or Being Levels. When the leader is at a Being Level, the team shifts toward a Being Level as well. They have no choice. This shifting of mindset becomes the true catalyst for behavioral change that will launch an organization into what we call a culture of action.

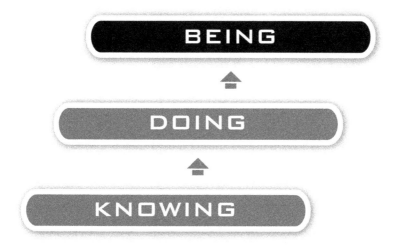

The Being Ladder shown above can be used to measure the level of a team's mindset and engagement to any specific initiative or even an organization's vision. Moving a team from the Doing Level to the Being Level in mindset is a critical component of success.

Leaders in key positions must achieve Being Level mindset for great success to take hold and become a part of the organization's culture. At the Being Level, Action Gaps are proactively closed and even prevented.

Winning leaders live at the Being Level in the important things.

Here are some things you must consider to become a winning leader and create a winning organization:

- What programs or processes are critical to the success of your organization?
- Where does your mindset reside, at the Knowing, Doing, or Being Level, in relation to these programs?
- If you say Being Level, would your team agree? Do they see Being Level when they look at your behavior?

We use an equation to predict the performance of an individual or a team. It has proven quite effective and quite accurate.

The equation is T x M = P.

T is for Talent, M is for Mindset or state of mind, and P is for Performance.

All leaders have a significant impact on mindset. We can't forget that. Winning leaders work hard to maintain a strong focus on their positive impact on mindset.

So, Talent (0-10) multiplied by Mindset (0-10) equals Performance Level (0-100). Interesting! This means that Talent and Mindset are equal in determining performance. We have found that no matter how talented an individual, their Mindset Level plays an equal role in their Performance over time. The individual's work/life balance, job satisfaction, issues at home, etc. can all impact Mindset and can be as important as their Talent Level!

The Dependence Ladder helps leaders understand the team member behavior that may be limiting their action and creating Action Gaps. Action will increase as a team member moves up the scale from dependence toward independence and finally to interdependence.

Here is the Dependence Ladder and descriptions of each level:

Dependence

Team members in this category need the support of others to fully execute their role. They drain the resources of the team.

Independence

These team members are fully functioning and may even prefer operating on their own. They will likely perform well and meet expectations.

Interdependence

This is the highest level of team member behavior. Team members who work interdependently share their successes and work for the betterment of the entire team, not just themselves. They seek win/win solutions

A culture of action is the desired outcome of Gapology and ultimately the difference between the winning leaders and the rest of the leaders we have studied.

Leader behaviors that initiate the culture of action:

- Identify and Close the Knowledge Gaps.
- Identify and Close the Importance Gaps.
- Identify and Close the Action Gaps. Build a support structure to proactively identify and close gaps.
- Seek team member feedback about their mindset and their Performance Gaps.
- Seek customer feedback on performance compared to their expectations.
- Respond to team member and customer feedback, perpetuating the culture of action.

Team member actions that are the outcome of leader behavior and continue the culture of action:

- Know and Do the expected behavior, achieving the desired outcomes.
- Achieve Doing Level engagement while working toward Being Level engagement.
- Give leader feedback to impact mindset.
- Give leader feedback on Performance Gaps.
- Share customer feedback with the leader.

Customer actions that result from team member execution, thus continuing the culture of action:

- Shift in spending patterns supporting desired behavior.
- Buying more and spending more.
- Increased frequency of purchasing.
- Create word of mouth about desired behaviors.
- Give feedback on experience.

The leader's behavior is the starting point for the culture of action. Winning leaders have learned how to create and sustain this culture.

NEXT STEPS

Teaching organizations are learning organizations. They are also winning organizations.

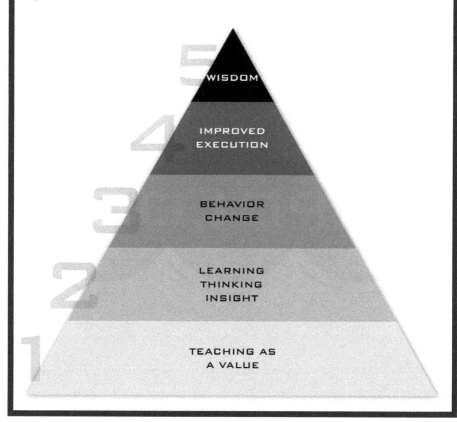

The Teaching Organization Pyramid model represents the power of developing a teaching organization and the ultimate goal of achieving organizational wisdom.

Most organizations do not qualify as teaching organizations because they often don't understand the value of teaching. They are built on a foundation of hierarchy or chain of command and may mistakenly believe that profit is all that matters.

Most organizations do not qualify as teaching organizations because they don't understand the value of leaders teaching. They may value learning, but that simply puts the ownership on the learner. It is much different to put the ownership on the leaders as teachers. Most organizations are built on a foundation of hierarchy or chain of command. Leaders stay out of the weeds, and the trainers' job is to teach. They mistakenly believe that the leaders aren't teachers, and their role is to simply drive profit.

Although profit is the reason for most organizations, an organization built on the foundation of teaching as a value can become a superior profit-generating organization as well.

When teaching becomes a value, and teachers are developed at all levels, the potential and sustainability of the organization become boundless.

259

QUOTABLE QUOTES FROM GAPOLOGY

- *"Gaps happen."*
- *"Gaps are everywhere."*
- *"Performance Gaps are the number-one risk to all companies and organizations today."*
- *"Winning leaders close Performance Gaps by taking action and moving their teams to take action."*
- *"Action speaks and performance screams, but results roar!"*
- *"Action is the key to beginning a cycle of achieving and exceeding expectations."*
- *"Gapology is the term we use to describe what winning leaders do to identify and close Performance Gaps in their teams."*
- *"The performance of the winning leaders is literally being canceled out by the poor performance of those not winning."*
- *"The sequential path winning leaders follow is what we call Gapology."*
- *"Regardless of their background, level of education, or geographic location, winning leaders consistently identify and then close Performance Gaps in themselves and their teams!"*
- *"All Performance Gaps are Knowledge, Importance, Action, or some combination of the three!"*

- *"Winning leaders ensure that their teams know 'what' actions to take, or 'what' is expected, and then 'how' to do it."*
- *"Winning leaders ensure that their teams know 'why' an action is important and 'when' it must be done."*
- *"Action Gaps mean that despite knowing 'what' to do and 'how' to do it, 'why' it is critical, and 'when' it must be done, the right actions are not taken."*
- *"Winning leaders know that Action Gaps are the most difficult to close and devote the time and attention necessary to ensure that they are closed airtight."*
- *"We found that Gapology is both the mindset and the leadership rhythm of winning leaders."*
- *"Gapology is a powerful tool that will transform team culture, creating a bias for action. It changes how individuals, teams and organizations think, speak, and behave."*
- *"Once you, as the leader of a team, become a true Gapologist, you can accomplish results far beyond your peers or competitors."*
- *"Once your eyes and your mind are open to Gapology, your life as a leader will be changed forever."*
- *"I see gaps…"*
- *"As a leader, you will often find that you are the gap."*
- *"Winning leaders make winning look easy, but that is often the outcome of significant learning through trial and error."*
- *"You can't close Action Gaps without Knowledge and Importance Gaps being closed."*
- *"Gapology is the bridge that leads from failure to success, and winning leaders cross that bridge many times each day."*
- *"Gapology is the most significant game-changer we have ever experienced."*

- *"Gapology is the most critical tool in a leader's toolbox."*
- *"Gapology will certainly change your results, and it has the power to change your life!"*
- *"Some leaders just assume that the behavior is known and therefore it will be sustained. This is a big mistake."*
- *"Performance Gaps ahead!"*
- *"Curiosity is a key quality of winning leaders, and it is a key to identifying gaps."*
- *"Gaps must first be identified if they are to be closed."*
- *"You can't close a gap you don't see!"*
- *"If you don't ask questions, you become the gap!"*
- *"Leaders who do not listen actively do not uncover gaps and are surprised when results miss expectations."*
- *"Many leaders jump to conclusions and assume too much, and this may cause them to work on closing gaps that are not the real issue."*
- *"Some leaders create more gaps than they close!"*
- *"Knowledge Gaps originate with the leader, so it up to the leader to close them."*
- *"Identifying and closing gaps quickly and permanently is a leader's role."*
- *"When your team is not performing to your expectations, start by looking in the mirror."*
- *"Assumption without verification creates a gap."*
- *"Telling ain't training!"*
- *"Recurring Knowledge Gaps by the same team member suggest that you have the wrong person in the role."*

- *"You may have heard the old saying, 'You can't teach an old dog new tricks.' This is true, unless you know how the old dog learns."*
- *"Great performance means minimizing the Knowledge Gaps not only with your team, but with your customers, too."*
- *"Winning leaders know that one of their primary roles is teaching."*
- *"The execution of any significant change is only as good as the leader's ability to explain it."*
- *"During times of change, leadership is the lighthouse in the fog of uncertainty. Winning leaders navigate the treacherous waters just fine, while the rest clearly struggle."*
- *"Winning leaders embrace change and know that it is the only constant."*
- *"Human behavior reacts to change very predictably, and it flows as follows: Denial, Anger, Bargaining, and then Acceptance."*
- *"Leaders are the most important catalyst in a team's path to acceptance of change."*
- *"Ultimately, the more talented and skilled the team you lead, the fewer Knowledge Gaps you will experience."*
- *"Talent matters, and putting the right person in the right role makes a huge difference in performance."*
- *"Winning leaders behavior when it comes to people moves is strategic and deliberate, thus, playing chess, not checkers."*
- *"Winning leaders know that the ideal team produces great results, is aligned with the organization's values, and has strong leadership, thus creating a bright future for the organization."*
- *"Winning leaders spend more personalized time with A-Players than any other group, followed by C-Players, then B."*

- *"Winning leaders share a philosophy of replacement leadership. They are always developing their replacement."*
- *"Talent creates talent, and with talent comes fewer Performance Gaps."*
- *"Winning leaders manage people unequally. They believe that leadership is not 'one size fits all,' and that it is more complex."*
- *"Too often, leaders focus solely on improving areas of their team members' weaknesses and completely ignore the areas where they excel."*
- *"Leaders need to make sure that the things that do inevitably fall through the cracks are never the big things."*
- *"Remember that Importance Gaps are created when someone knows what needs to be done and knows how to do it, but they don't take action because they don't feel, consciously or subconsciously, that it is important enough."*
- *"Importance Gaps are owned by the leader and are most often caused by a leader's lack of clarity."*
- *"The power of understanding and executing Gapology is that you can close specific gaps that can't be reopened."*
- *"Gapology will shed light on gaps that you may not have been looking for."*
- *"Recurring Knowledge and Importance Gaps highlight possible performance issues."*
- *"In the absence of a leader's clarity about what is important, chaos fills the gap, and that chaos leads to gaps in productivity and performance."*
- *"Many leaders make the mistake of setting goals but not expectations. Winning leaders know to do both."*

- *"Expectations are the things that the leader 'expects' to be delivered and are nonnegotiable."*
- *"Winning leaders are confident that when the behavioral component of an expectation is met, the result component will follow."*
- *"Winning leaders know that there is no substitute for setting clear expectations."*
- *"One Knowledge or Importance Gap that is often missed is the one with your boss."*
- *"Just like recurring Knowledge Gaps imply a talent issue with a team member, recurring Importance Gaps imply a clarity and prioritization issue with the leader. There tends to be an overriding assumption by leaders who miss expectations that if something has been communicated, it is therefore understood and will be acted upon."*
- *"Winning leaders assume nothing!"*
- *"Winning leaders leverage communication as a differentiator. It closes gaps."*
- *"Clear, concise, and verified communication closes Importance Gaps."*
- *"Winning leadership rhythm is the consistent and predictable way winning leaders behave."*
- *"Winning leaders make mistakes, but what separates them is that they learn from their mistakes, adjusting their leadership and direction to win."*
- *"We don't have hard proof, but we believe that winning leaders make more mistakes than others because they take more risks. Playing it safe rarely leads to winning."*
- *"Closed Knowledge Gaps and Importance Gaps set up teams to win!"*

- *"Winning leaders put up the scoreboard, fill the seats with screaming fans, and have a front-row seat at the fifty-yard line."*
- *"Creating a culture that keeps score creates a culture of action."*
- *"If everything is important, nothing is important."*
- *"Most gaps are caused by inaction. Clear priorities create action."*
- *"Leader behavior and actions must reflect the priorities."*
- *"Shared vision is about alignment of purpose. When a team has a shared vision, it operates as one."*
- *"Less is more when it comes to the focuses of a high performance team. The fewer things on which you are focused, the greater the focus on each."*
- *"Action Gaps in the behavior of leaders are unacceptable to winning leaders because they know that these gaps create much bigger gaps downstream."*
- *"There is a big difference between action and performance. When you get your team to take the right action, that action equals performance, and performance achieves the desired results."*
- *"Remember… Busy ain't productive!"*
- *"Don't confuse being busy with being productive. Busy is action, but true productivity is performance (right action) that delivers desired results. Many people have simply learned to look productive."*
- *"Winning leaders create accountability. They use a variety of different ways to do this, but the old-fashioned way still works best. They simply set clear expectations and follow up."*
- *"Winning leaders create accountability by transferring ownership of their own plays to others."*

- *"Winning leaders use EDGE to create action and accountability."*
- *"EDGE can be described as a strong point of view or belief in something. It is being unwavering and showing unwillingness to compromise on values and standards."*
- *"Progress is good, but celebrating it may inhibit achieving the expectations."*
- *"A winning leader taught us the analogy that progress is like driving a car down a long highway and looking in the rearview mirror to see how far you have come. Expectations, where you are going, are not visible in the rearview mirror."*
- *"A bad attitude does not stand a chance of surviving winning leadership. So, when there is a bad attitude on your team, take another close look in the mirror and make sure you have applied the steps to close the gap. Bad attitudes either change or run away from winning leaders."*
- *"Winning leaders transfer ownership for expectations to the individual who is responsible for the performance."*
- *"Borrowing power results in failure."*
- *"Leaders and team members who are committed or genuinely compliant to the vision of an organization will have fewer Action Gaps and will likely close them before they happen."*
- *"Winning leaders trump the company. People work for people more than they work for companies."*
- *"Winning leaders develop people, and if they are especially skilled and diligent in this effort, they develop people whom they may someday work for."*
- *"A shift in the mindset of the leader creates lasting behavior change within a team. If you do not have the desired culture of action in your organization, you likely need a behavioral change to occur, beginning with the mindset of leadership."*

- *"Behavioral change needs to be intentional, and it is the catalyst to transforming an organization into something that it is not today."*
- *"Being is like Doing squared."*
- *"T x M = P."*
- *"Winning leaders work hard to have a positive impact on the mindset of their team."*
- *"Winning leaders excel at developing the skills and increasing the talent of their team."*
- *"Change everything, and everything will change."*
- *"Winning leaders have learned how to create and sustain a culture of action."*
- *"Teaching organizations are capable of creating results that other companies admire from afar and can't comprehend. Teaching creates energy in both the teacher and in the learner that makes work exciting."*
- *"The success of winning leaders is built upon teaching as a competency, a passion, and a part of their daily rhythm."*
- *"Teaching as a value becomes contagious and creates a culture of teaching that can potentially lead to organizational wisdom."*
- *"Learning and thinking are competitive advantages for organizations because learning and thinking create insight."*

SOURCES OF INSPIRATION

Anderson, D., & Ackerman, Anderson, L. (2001). *Beyond Change Management.* Hoboken, NJ: Wiley, John and Sons, Inc.

Argyris, C., & Schon, D. A. (1992). *Theory in Practice: Increasing Professional Effectiveness.* Hoboken, NJ: Wiley, John and Sons, Inc.

Buckingham, M., & Clifton, D. O. (2001). *Now, Discover Your Strengths.* New York, NY: The Free Press—Division of Simon & Schuster, Inc.

Collins, J. (2001). *Good to Great.* New York, NY: HarperCollins Publishers.

Kolb, D. A. (1983). *Experiential Learning: Experience as the Source of Learning and Development.* Englewood Cliffs, NJ: Prentice Hall.

Senge, P. M. (2006). *The Fifth Discipline: The Art and Practice of the Learning Organization.* New York, NY: Doubleday.

Tichy, N. M., & Cardwell, N. (2004). *The Cycle of Leadership: How Great Leaders Teach Their Companies to Win.* New York, NY: HarperCollins Publishers.

272

FIGURES

274

INDEX

ACKNOWLEDGMENTS

As we look back over the years at everything we have learned, we realize that we have been extremely blessed.

We want to thank just a few of the teachers who helped shape our leadership. Winning leaders like Garry and Larry Remington, Gary White, Judy Shoulak, Becky Mick, Karla Artz, Karen Schultz, and so many others have shown us the way while being mentors as well.

Then there were the coaches and consultants who helped shape our leadership philosophies and tactics: Roger Merrill, Barry Rellaford, Tom Riskas, and Mark's coach and mentor, Mark Maraia. To them, we owe a large debt of gratitude.

We would also like to give special recognition to our families. Our wives, Darla and Jolyann, have provided the perfect balance of encouragement and support while being the shoulders to lean on and the voices of reason throughout this journey. We thank our children, Jason, Bryan, Courtney, Jesse, Jonas, and Jacob, for being "okay" with their dads' mysterious absences and for giving us love and encouragement when we return.

And, finally, we would like to thank all of the "Maddys" we've had the pleasure of working with. These teams and winning leaders have given us the inspiration and motivation to tackle this endeavor. We have learned and continue to learn from them each day. We hope that, through this book, we can return the favor.

280

ENDORSEMENTS

"I read every word of Gapology *and found a hundred ways to apply its wisdom to my classroom and to my students. Unlike all the other leadership books I've read,* Gapology *seeks to understand why we succeed, why we fail, and why the gap between the two can seem so impossibly wide or so frustratingly narrow. The day after I finished this book, my classroom got even better, and the results are pouring in!"*—**Josh Anderson, Head Coach, Olathe Northwest High School Debate and Forensics, 2007 Kansas Teacher of the Year, 2007 National Teacher of the Year, Runner-Up**

I am a current Vice President of Retail Operations for Goodwill in the Figure Lakes in New York. I have also held Vice President of Retail positions in OfficeMax and Sears Holdings for Kmart. The Gapology *concepts, theories and behaviors apply to successfully improving results in profit and non-profit organizations. Successful leaders that consistently practice them in a systemic approach find themselves producing higher results than those that do not. I have seen the significantly improved business results that follow retail leaders tenaciously closing Performance Gaps. Run the numbers for your business, whether you're running a store, district, region or greater, it is amazing to see the additional profit you can deliver for your business when you close the gaps."*—**Paul Geisler, Vice President, Retail Fortune 500**

"Throughout my career, Mark Thienes has always inspired me to achieve greatness. It is rare to find a book that relates to the retail industry as well as Gapology *does. It captures the formulas of the winning leaders and puts them in a simple context for executives at any level. It teaches leaders how to identify Performance Gaps and take the right action to close those gaps -- both in their leadership and in their teams. Over the years, as an executive, it has been an absolute pleasure to watch my team put* Gapology *concepts to practice, allowing them to achieve consistent optimal results. The process is a rewarding journey to say the least; the enthusiasm and heightened performance following* Gapology's *influence has been incomparable."* **Roselyn Hammond, Regional Director - Store Operations, 99 Cent Only Stores LLC, City of Commerce, CA**

"*Gapology is an incredibly interesting journey through the thought process of what makes a winning business sales team successful. The book teaches how to identify 'gaps' of performance expectations and business understanding in any business and provides valuable lessons on how to fill those 'gaps.' The principles of the lessons are truly applicable to any division of any company. We apply the lessons of Gapology to our business every day to inspire every employee to be the best they can be. Gapology provides invaluable insight into how to make your company more effective and profitable.*" -**Steve Hoffman, CEO, TradingBlock.com**

"*At all levels of management, the most common question asked is, 'Why doesn't everyone understand my vision for the organization?' At all levels of supervisory relationships, the answer has arrived. The gaps! Gapology will show you how to identify what your people know versus what you thought they knew. This book was written by tried-and-true retail professionals, people who lived and breathed these methods and excelled in the process. These methods will change the way you manage your team and change the way your team views you. Give it a try; you'll be building a stronger team.*"—**Bill Jenkins, Group Director, Retail Development, *NEW* Customer Service Companies, Inc.**

"*Reading Gapology was a thunderclap—we discovered that we were the problem with our faltering business. We had a talented team, but we had failed to close their Knowledge Gaps with teaching and training, and by clearly conveying expectations with Gapology we are well on the way to producing 'results that roar.'*"—**Carl and Susan Lyday, Small Business Owners**

"*Mark Thienes has written a book that all winning leaders will gain insight from reading. It explains in simple terms what your organization can do to close any and all Performance Gaps. You'll want every member of your team to learn and apply the principles in this book.*"—**Mark M. Maraia, Executive Coach and Author of *Rainmaking Made Simple* and *Relationships Are Everything!***

"*I was introduced to Gapology approximately ten years ago and it totally changed my thought process in how to manage processes and people. Gapology is designed not only for front line management but executive leadership as well. I have found myself referring back to the Performance Gap methodology many times in my career. In my opinion, there is no other management tool out there that clearly defines not only how to determine why a gap may exists, but more importantly, how to fill the gap to get the desired results you are trying to obtain. I highly recommend reading and embracing Gapology. It will change the way you manage your business.*" —**Steve McKinley, Division Vice President of a Specialty Retailer with Over $3 Billion in Revenue**

"I read Gapology *over the weekend. I started it this morning after breakfast and just finished. I couldn't put it down. I found it brilliantly written, insightful, and a lot of fun to read. It is the best business/management 'self-improvement' book I've read in years."*—**Garry Remington, President, GJ Remington Consulting, LLC, Former Senior Vice President, Foot Locker, Senior Vice President, Mrs. Fields Famous Brands**

"I just finished Gapology, *and as Garry had warned me…I couldn't put it down until it was finished! The stories, the examples, the illustrations, the charts, Maddy's learnings, and the* Gapology *lessons all made this a must-read and a memorable learning experience. Anyone interested in WINNING needs to follow the* Gapology *method and start building a Culture of Action!!!"*—**Larry Remington, President CEO K-Swiss Global Brands**

"Transformative is the word that best comes to mind when I think about the impact of Gapology *on my organization. This transformation establishes itself first within the leadership of the business as they begin to read & understand that a culture of simply treating the symptoms of a gap does nothing to ensure the long-term growth of the people or the business as a whole. Mark & Brian have established a clear path on how to not only identify gaps, but more importantly pinpoint the root cause of the gap itself and close it through ownership & accountability. I wish I had a resource like this when I started my career, it would have prevented a lot of tough lessons learned over the years."* — **Jeff Ronald, Vice President of Sales & Operations RW & Co.**

*"*Gapology *is simply… BRILLIANT! This is clearly a bold statement, but the truth is,* Gapology *is worthy of every letter in that bold statement. The clear, easily under-stood, and common sense of the methodology behind* Gapology *applies to all aspects of our lives. That is what is so great about it! Mark Thienes and Brian Brockhoff have gifted us with a book that helps us dance with personal challenges and decisions, as well as a process for success professionally. I have spent 20 years dancing with a life changing illness, and one of my greatest lessons is: If I want different results and to live a fulfilled and vital life, I need to identify my 'gaps' and create change. I was doing pretty good on my own, and then enter stage left… Gapology. What a gift! I was able to step into a new level of responsibility in my journey to find myself and heal. Success happens when we find our gaps."* —**Kimberly Rooney, Author of** *Spiritual Two-by-Fours and Other Wake-up Calls*

"Mark Thienes has applied 30+ years of managerial and interpersonal business experience into a practical and usable model for growth -- predicated on the age old axiom that resolving a problem begins with correctly identifying and accepting it. The elegance of his model is that it is simple enough to be equally applicable on an individual and organizational level, making it usable in corporate, academic, and even family environments."— **Dr. Greg Salsbury, President, Western State Colorado University**

"Performance sounds so simple, but obviously it is not. With so many areas of a business involved, it is challenging to identify where the breakdown is occurring. Mark Thienes and Brian Brockhoff break this complex process into very simple pieces. Gapology provides a very methodical and logical approach to identifying and closing the gaps in performance. This book is worth reading and keeping handy as a reference guide!"— **Judy Shoulak, EVP, President North America, Buffalo Wild Wings**

"Gapology is a lifestyle that I have embraced after reading the book roughly three years ago and continue to develop and apply in my career and my life to date. This book has helped me understand Knowledge, Importance, and Action Gaps and also gave me the ability to recognize and close those gaps with employees and even my children. The content and thoughts behind Gapology are great for young and aspiring leaders as well as seasoned leadership who are further looking to develop their skills. Since applying Gapology, I have led best in class teams and accomplished goals in a very short period of time. If you are looking to take your team, career, and leadership to the next level, read Gapology and apply it!" — **Michael Shultz, Warehouse Manager, Uline**

"Gapology has absolutely become a part of our culture. The concepts are easy to understand (as compared to, say, Six Sigma). Having a common language makes it easy for our larger team to quickly understand what's happening (the type of gap) and what we're doing (the Root Solution), particularly when we have very different roles within the team. Managing a training organization, the Habit Ladder has become a part of every initial analysis; we create learning objectives based on what we determine needs to be at the Habit Level when a learner leaves our training. Highly recommended!" —**Kathy Straley, Retail Payment Solutions, Employee Engagement Group Manager, Banking Fortune 500**

"Gapology is at the heart of problem solving methodology. Mark keys in on the core elements that make or break performance success in any organization. Once you learn and understand how Gapology works, you will want to apply it and see the results unfold!" —**Robert R. Vandercook, Jr., Founder eryoodition, LLC.**

ABOUT THE AUTHORS

Mark Thienes' journey encompasses thirty years of success in leading teams to winning seasons. He proudly refers to himself as "The Original Gapologist" and is the founder of Gapology.

Great authors such as Peter Senge, Chris Argyris, Noel Tichy, and David Kolb have had a major impact on his leadership philosophies. His personal passion is developing winning leaders.

Mark's first and favorite question for winning leaders is, "How did you do that?" He loves to hear their thought processes and the tactics deployed to win. Gapology is about creating winning leaders. Mark resides in Colorado and is a native Californian.

Brian Brockhoff has led, trained, and coached teams of diverse business leaders for over twenty years and is responsible for the creation and design of numerous skill development programs. He has authored a book of weekly inspirations based on the principles described here entitled *Gapology Inspirations*, and he writes regularly on Wordpress.com.

Brian is a cofounder of Gapology and a Gapology coach. Originally from Minneapolis, Minnesota, he now lives with his family in Kansas City, Kansas.

CONNECT
WITH GAPOLOGY

Email Mark or Brian for training coaching or speaking events:

markthienes@gapologyinstitute.com

brianbrockhoff@gapologyinstitute.com

Follow Gapology on Social Media:

LINKEDIN

www.linkedin.com/in/markthienes

www.linkedin.com/in/brianbrockhoff

FACEBOOK

facebook.com/gapologyinstitute

TWITTER

@gapology

For training material and other books visit:

WWW.GAPOLOGYINSTITUTE.COM

CPSIA information can be obtained
at www.ICGtesting.com
Printed in the USA
BVHW01s1744080218
507489BV00002B/134/P